English through the News Media

—2021 Edition—

Masami Takahashi
Noriko Itoh
Richard Powell

Asahi Press

記事提供
The New York Times
The Times
The Japan Times
The Guardian
Bloomberg
Evening Standard
The Express & Star
Kyodo
AFP-JIJI

写真提供
アフロ：The New York Times／Redux／Erickson production／
ロイター／Splash／picture alliance／AP／TT News Agency／
新華社／Alamy／ED／JL／A.M.P.A.S.／Camera Press／Rex／
Kyodo News

地図・イラスト
ヨシオカユリ

English through the News Media —2021 Edition—
Copyright © 2021 by Asahi Press

は　し　が　き

　本書は、世界のニュースを通して Reading, Listening, Speaking, Writing のバランスの
とれた学習が効果的にできるように工夫してあります。2019年5月：上流階級育ちの
坊ちゃんの中身のない自信に気をつけろ、8月：渋野日向子、全英女子オープンゴル
フ優勝でメジャーデビュー；独立20年後、経済的困窮の東ティモールに中国が援助の
手を、10月：ラグビー「桜戦士」、チームの結束を称賛；日本のファンは歴史的成果を
褒めちぎる；iPhoneのはるか前に無線社会の基礎を築いた人たち；超人間的なAIは御免
だ；ハイチ、崖っぷちに追い込まれる；「飛び恥」が航空業界に打撃、11月：日本の報
道機関、自国の将来に確信が無い；コアラが森林火災の犠牲に；ロシアの科学者、安全
保障上の強制捜査のショック；英語教育改革を凍結させてはいけない、12月：フィンラ
ンドで世界最年少首相が誕生；ノート型パソコンのリサイクルでの代償：タイで有毒ガ
スが；生徒の読解力を測る国際的試験で日本は過去最低の水準に落ちた；移民流入は壁
では阻止できない；新国籍法への反対運動が荒れ狂うが、インドはヒンドゥ教国となる
のか、2020年1月：サウジ社会の変化はコーヒーハウスを覗けば分かる；カルロス・ゴ
ーンの大脱走劇、2月：ソマリアの若者たち、政府機能不全の地域に足を踏み入れる；
特殊メイクのカズ・ヒロさん、二度目のアカデミー賞；韓国映画『パラサイト』がアカ
デミー賞受賞、3月：英国、デジタル技術要員養成へ；疫病時にはアジア人でなくても
マスクした方がいいのか；疫病の渦中で必要なのはフランスではペストリーとワイン、
米国ではゴルフと銃；フィンランド「世界で最も幸せな国」の王座維持；ギリシャの難
民秘密収容所では「まるで動物扱い」、4月：eスポーツがオリンピック後の日本を救う
か？；他の人たちよりもずっと感染力が強い人たちがいる理由；急激な変化：ガイアナ
は石油で裕福になったが、民族間の緊張も増大、まで世界中のニュースを満載しており
ます。

　*The New York Times, The New York Times International Edition, The Japan Times, Evening
Standard, The Guardian, The Times, The Express & Star* から社会・文化・政治経済・情
報・言語・教育・科学・医学・環境・娯楽・スポーツなどのあらゆる分野を網羅しまし
たので、身近に世界中のニュースに触れ、読み、聞き、話し、書く楽しさを育みなが
ら、多角的にそして複眼的に英語運用力が自然に培われるように意図しています。

　26課より構成され、各課に新聞記事読解前にBefore you readを設けました。本文の内
容が予想できる写真と、どこにあるかを示す地図と国の情報を参照しながら自由に意見
交換をします。次の Words and Phrases では、記事に記載されている単語や熟語とそれに
合致する英語の説明を選び、あらかじめ大事な語の理解を深めて行きます。Summaryで
は記事の内容を予想しながら、5語を適当な箇所に記入して要約文を完成させます。記

事読解前では難しいようであれば、読解後に活用しても良いと思います。さらに、記事に関連した裏話も載せました。記事の読解にあたり、わかり易い註釈を記事の右端に付け、理解度をチェックするための Multiple Choice, True or False, 記事に関連した語法を学ぶVocabularyと豊富に取り揃えました。Summaryと記事がそのまま音声化されたファイルをウェブ上にあげています。多方面に渡る記事やExercisesを活用して、英字新聞に慣れ親しみ、使っていただけることを望んでいます。

　今回テキスト作成に際して、お世話になりました朝日出版社社長原雅久氏、編集部の日比野忠氏、小川洋一郎氏に心からお礼申し上げます。

2020年10月

高橋　優身

伊藤　典子

Richard Powell

CONTENTS

＊印の15章を *15 Selected Units of English Through the News Media —2021 Edition—* として別途刊行しています。

English through the News Media -2021 Edition-

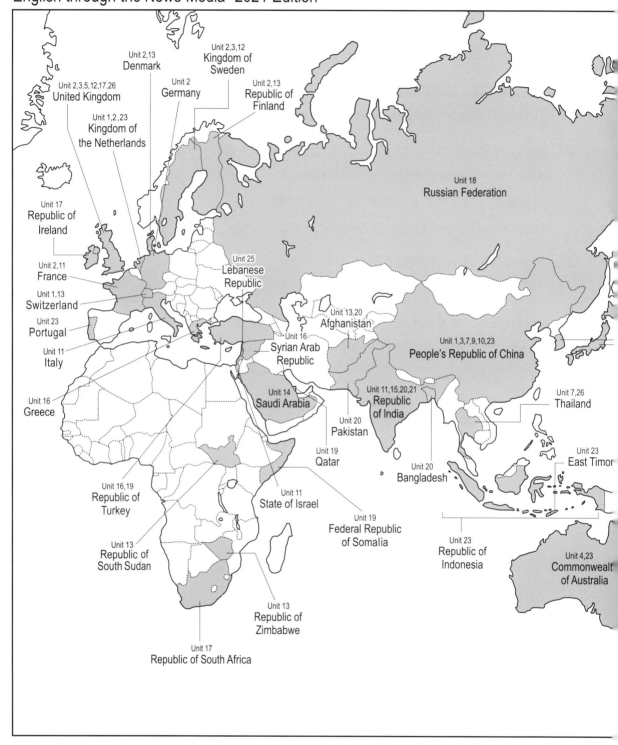

Unit 2,13
Denmark

Unit 2,3,12
Kingdom of
Sweden

Unit 2
Germany

Unit 2,13
Republic of
Finland

Unit 2,3,5,12,17,26
United Kingdom

Unit 1,2,23
Kingdom of
the Netherlands

Unit 17
Republic of
Ireland

Unit 18
Russian Federation

Unit 25
Lebanese
Republic

Unit 2,11
France

Unit 1,13
Switzerland

Unit 13,20
Afghanistan

Unit 23
Portugal

Unit 16
Syrian Arab
Republic

Unit 1,3,7,9,10,23
People's Republic of China

Unit 11
Italy

Unit 16
Greece

Unit 14
Saudi Arabia

Unit 11,15,20,21
Republic
of India

Unit 7,26
Thailand

Unit 20
Pakistan

Unit 19
Qatar

Unit 23
East Timor

Unit 16,19
Republic of
Turkey

Unit 11
State of Israel

Unit 20
Bangladesh

Unit 19
Federal Republic
of Somalia

Unit 23
Republic of
Indonesia

Unit 4,23
Commonwealt
of Australia

Unit 13
Republic of
South Sudan

Unit 13
Republic of
Zimbabwe

Unit 17
Republic of South Africa

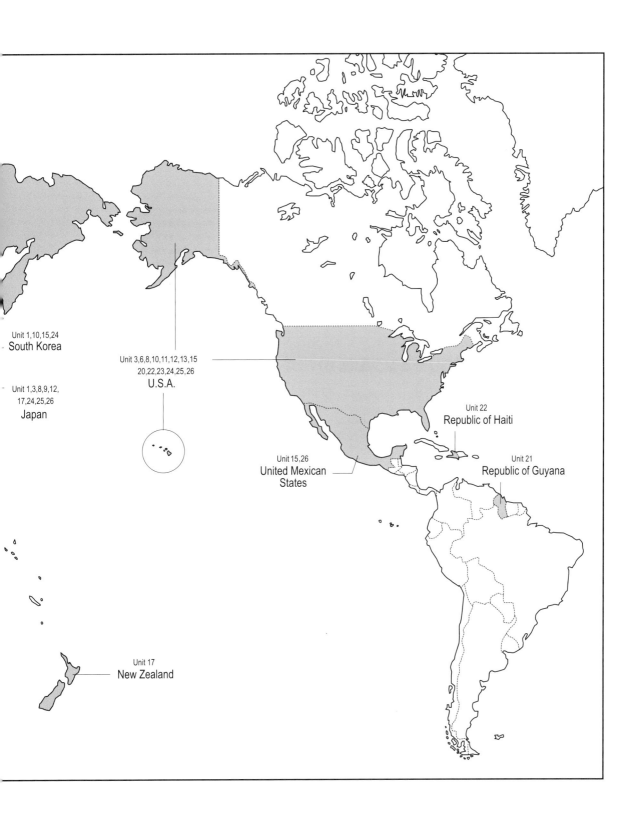

Unit 1,10,15,24
South Korea

Unit 1,3,8,9,12,
17,24,25,26
Japan

Unit 3,6,8,10,11,12,13,15
20,22,23,24,25,26
U.S.A.

Unit 22
Republic of Haiti

Unit 21
Republic of Guyana

Unit 15,26
United Mexican
States

Unit 17
New Zealand

音声再生アプリ「リスニング・トレーナー」を使った音声ダウンロード

朝日出版社開発のアプリ、「リスニング・トレーナー（リストレ）」を使えば、教科書の音声をスマホ、タブレットに簡単にダウンロードできます。どうぞご活用ください。

◉ アプリ【リスニング・トレーナー】の使い方

《アプリのダウンロード》

App Store または Google Play から「リスニング・トレーナー」のアプリ（無料）をダウンロード

App Storeはこちら▶

Google Playはこちら▶

《アプリの使い方》

① アプリを開き「コンテンツを追加」をタップ
② 画面上部に【15663】を入力しDoneをタップ

音声ストリーミング配信 ≫≫

この教科書の音声は、右記ウェブサイトにて無料で配信しています。

https://text.asahipress.com/free/english/

English through the News Media

●英語教育改革を凍結させてはいけない

●生徒の読解力を測る国際的試験で日本は過去最低水準に落ちた

平均得点の国際比較

順位	科学的応用力		読解力		数学的応用力	
1	(10)北京・上海・江蘇・浙江※	590	(27)北京・上海・江蘇・浙江※	555	(6)北京・上海・江蘇・浙江※	591
2	(1)シンガポール	551	(1)シンガポール	549	(1)シンガポール	569
3	(6)マ カ オ	544	(12)マ カ オ	525	(3)マ カ オ	558
4	(3)エストニア	530	(2)香　港	524	(2)香　港	551
5	(2)日　本	529	(6)エストニア	523	(4)台　湾	531
6	(5)フィンランド	522	(3)カ ナ ダ	520	(5)日　本	527
7	(11)韓　国	519	(4)フィンランド	520	(7)韓　国	526
8	(7)カ ナ ダ	518	(5)アイルランド	518	(9)エストニア	523
9	(9)香　港	517	(7)韓　国	514	(11)オ ラ ン ダ	519
10	(4)台　湾	516	(13)ポーランド	512	(17)ポーランド	516
	OECD平均	489	15 (8)日　本	504	OECD平均	489
			OECD平均	487		

（　）は前回順位、小数点以下は四捨五入、※前回は北京・上海・江蘇・広東として参加

日本の読解力15位、上位層と差を示す PISA の平均得点の国際比較
Photo: Kyodo News

Before you read

Japan　日本国

面積　377,961.73km²（世界61位）
人口　126,860,000人（世界11位）
　　　日本民族　98.5%
　　　朝鮮人　0.5%
　　　中国人　0.4%
首都　東京都
最大都市　大阪市（昼間人口）
　　　　　横浜市（夜間人口）
　　　　　東京都23区部
GDP　4兆9,718億ドル（世界３位）
　　　１人当たりの GDP　39,304ドル
　　　　　　　　　　　　　　（世界26位）

通貨　円
公用語　なし、事実上日本語
宗教　無宗教信者　52%
　　　仏教　35%　/　神道　４%
　　　キリスト教　2.3%
政治　立憲君主制
識字率　99.8%

Words and Phrases

次の１～５の語の説明として最も近いものをa～eから１つ選び、（　）内に記入しなさい。

1. assess	（　）	**a.**	achievement or skill
2. discriminate	（　）	**b.**	join or be involved
3. proficiency	（　）	**c.**	trustworthiness
4. credibility	（　）	**d.**	evaluate or measure
5. participate	（　）	**e.**	treat unfairly

Summary

次の英文は記事の要約です。下の語群から最も適切な語を１つ選び、（　）内に記入しなさい。

1-02

Although still above the OECD (　　　　　), Japan dropped seven places in international (　　　　　) for reading skills. Students appear to be especially poor at reading long (　　　　　) on computers. There was even worse news for English skills, with one body (　　　　　) Japan 53 out of 100. Meanwhile the Ministry of Education is (　　　　　) to reform university entrance exams.

average　　placing　　rankings　　struggling　　texts

2020年度からスタートする大学入学共通テストで、英語民間試験の活用が見送られることになった。試験に向けて努力を積み重ねてきた高校生の間には、困惑が広がっている。

大学入試センター試験に代わる大学入学共通テストは、小中高校教育の転換も目指していて、中心が数学や国語への記述式問題採用と英語の「読む・聞く・話す・書く」の４技能を測る民間試験の活用だった。英検、TOEFL iBT, GTEC, TEAP, TEAP CBT, IELTS, Cambridge の７種類の英語民間試験から、受験生本人が選び、４月から12月の間に２回まで受けることができる。この英語民間試験を活用するには、実施会場が都市部に偏り、地方在住の受験生には負担が大きい、また受験料が高額で２回で約５万円もかかる、試験の難易度が異なり複数試験の比較が難しい、試験ごとに異なる採点基準、不正や機器トラブルなどへの対応など課題が山積みである。文科省は、英語入学試験を2024年度開始と掲げているが、生徒が身に着けた英語力をきちんと評価できる試験を検討してもらいたい。

OECD が79か国・地域の15歳計約60万人を対象に2018年に実施した PISA 国際学習到達度調査の結果を公表したが、日本は「読解力」が15位で2015年の８位から大きく順位を下げた。正答率が低かったのは、文章から必要な情報を探り出したり、文章の信用性を吟味したりする問題だった。スマートフォンの普及により、仲間同士の短文や絵文字のやりとりが中心になり、長い文章をきちんと読む機会が減っているのも原因の１つだ。

Reading

1-03

Don't freeze English education reform

The government last week announced it was putting off the planned introduction of private-sector English proficiency tests as part of standardized university entrance exams next April after the new system was criticized for many problems 5 regarding access to testing locations and higher examination fees.

The current English-language component of the standardized entrance exams only assesses reading and listening comprehension. By using private-sector tests that also check 10 writing and speaking ability, there were great expectations that students would be evaluated in a more comprehensive manner and thereby would prepare better to communicate in English.

1-04

Under the proposed system, six private-sector institutions 15 were to provide seven kinds of tests, including the GTEC (Global Test of English Communication), TOEFL, Cambridge English test and Japan's Eiken test starting next April.

But some critics said the new system would discriminate against students in remote areas because not all of the 20 proficiency tests would be offered in every prefecture. The fees for taking the exams also varied, with some costing over ¥20,000. This meant students from wealthy families and those living in big cities will have had an advantage.

In recent years, China, South Korea and many other non-25 English speaking countries have been pushing hard to enhance their English education, and as a result their skills appear to have improved dramatically.

1-05

English proficiency rankings illustrate this trend. A 2019 study by EF Education First, a Switzerland-based company 30 that offers language training, ranked the Netherlands at the top of 100 countries surveyed. Looking at Asian countries, Japan came in at a lowly 53rd, far behind South Korea at 37th

---

putting off ～：～を延期する

introduction：導入

private-sector：民間の

proficiency tests：検定試験

standardized：共通の

component：構成要素

comprehensive：総合的な

GTEC：ジーテック《ベネッセコーポレーションが実施している英語4技能検定》

TOEFL：トフル《第2言語としての英語のテスト；米国大学や大学院に入学希望する外国人用》

Cambridge English test：ケンブリッジ英検《ケンブリッジ大学英語検定機構が実施》

Eiken test：英検《日本英語検定協会が実施》

discriminate against ～：～に不公平な取り扱いをする

pushing hard：大いに推進する

enhance ～：～を強化する

EF Education First：イーエフ《1965年、スウェーデンで創立の私立語学学校》

---

and China at 40th.

The Japan Times, November 8, 2019

1-06

In international test, Japan sinks to lowest-ever rank for students' reading skills

In a triennial international survey on academic ability, Japanese students ranked at their lowest level ever for reading skills while remaining in the top band for science and mathematics, the OECD said Tuesday.

The 2018 Program for International Student Assessment tests covered about 600,000 15-year-old students in 79 countries and regions.

Japanese students came 15th in reading — down from eighth in the 2015 tests.

They scored 504 points on average for reading skills, which was higher than the average score of 487 among the 37 OECD members, but down by 12 points from the previous test.

1-07
The education ministry believes students can still improve in their ability to find information from texts, as well as better evaluate the credibility of texts and more clearly explain their thoughts and reasoning to others. It also pointed out that Japanese students are not used to reading long passages on computer screens.

Students in Japan also ranked lower for science — in fifth place, down from second — and mathematics — at sixth, down from fifth.

Beijing, Shanghai, Jiangsu province and Zhejiang province, which jointly participated in the tests as one region, finished first in the three fields. Singapore, which came first in the 2015 tests, ranked second in the three categories.

The Japan Times based on JIJI, December 4, 2019

triennial：３年に一度の

academic ability：学力

science：理科

OECD：経済協力開発機構

Program for International Student Assessment：生徒の学習到達度調査 (PISA)

education ministry：文部科学省

credibility：信頼性

reasoning：推論

are not used to ～ ing：～することに慣れていない

Beijing：北京

Jiangsu province：江蘇省

Zhejiang province：浙江省

fields：分野

categories：部門《fields と同じ》

Exercises

Multiple Choice

次の１～４の英文を完成させ、５の英文の質問に答えるために、ａ～ｄの中から最も適切なものを１つ選びなさい。

1. The article about 'English education reform' states that
    a. private sector English proficiency tests are creative and will work well for students.
    b. the high fees are a guarantee for acquiring greater students.
    c. these tests are located in very convenient facilities.
    d. there were plans for more comprehensive testing.

2. The top country for English proficiency according to the 2019 study was
    a. the Netherlands.
    b. Switzerland.
    c. South Korea.
    d. China.

3. The International Student Assessment was given to:
    a. 20,000 students.
    b. 60,000 students.
    c. 200,000 students.
    d. 600,000 students.

4. A problem that the lowered test scores may reflect was
    a. students' discomfort at reading long passages on computer screens.
    b. poor directions by the administrator.
    c. crowded testing sites in distant areas.
    d. expensive exam fees.

5. How many different English-language skills were to be tested in students?
    a. Two.
    b. Four.
    c. Five.
    d. Seven.

本文の内容に合致するものに T（True）、合致しないものに F（False）をつけなさい。

(   ) **1.** Japanese students had disappointing scores on the International Students Assessment tests.

(   ) **2.** The country that finished first in reading, mathematics, and science is Singapore.

(   ) **3.** South Korea has been pushing to enhance their English education.

(   ) **4.** The government planned to take out English reading and listening tests and replace them with speaking and writing ability tests.

(   ) **5.** The new plan for testing will continue as scheduled next April.

Vocabulary

次の１〜８は、「read」に関する英文です。日本文に合わせて（   ）内に最も適切な語を下の語群から１つ選び、記入しなさい。

1. 母は、私たちによく読み聞かせをしてくれた。
Our mother used to read (   ) us.

2. 友人が肝臓ガンで亡くなったことを新聞で知った。
I read (   ) the paper that my friend died of a liver cancer.

3. 手相を見ましょうか？
Can I (   ) your palm?

4. 彼女の答えは、辞退だと思った。
I read her reply (   ) a refusal.

5. 行間を読む必要がある。
You have to read (   ) the lines.

6. 娘は、４歳なのに文字がよく読める。
My daughter reads (   ) for a four-year-old.

7. その議事録を読まれたものとみなして良いだろう。
We can (   ) the minutes as read.

8. 朝１時間読書するのを習慣にしている。
I (   ) a rule of reading an hour in the morning.

as	between	in	make
read	take	to	well

Unit 2

●英国、デジタル技術要員養成へ

科学技術はほとんどの人々の仕事方法を急速に、そして根本的に変えつつあり、仕事の「本質」は粉砕され、新種のデジタルスキルに対する需要が増大している

Photo: Erickson production ／アフロ

Before you read

the United Kingdom of Great Britain and Northern Ireland
英国（グレートブリテン及び北アイルランド連合王国）

面積　244,820km²（日本の本州と四国とほぼ同じ）
　　　（世界78位）
人口　67,530,000人（世界21位）
公用語　英語
首都　ロンドン
民族　イングランド人　5,500万人
　　　スコットランド人　540万人
　　　（北）アイルランド人　181万人
　　　ウエールズ人　300万人
宗教　キリスト教　71.6%／イスラム教徒　2.7%
　　　ヒンドゥ教　1.0%
GDP　２兆8,288億ドル（世界５位）
　　　１人当たり GDP　42,580ドル（世界22位）
通貨　UK ポンド
政体　立憲君主制
識字率　99%

次の１〜５の語の説明として最も近いものをa〜eから１つ選び、（　）内に記入しなさい。

1. expertise   (　　)   **a.** formatting for computer use
2. digitalization   (　　)   **b.** confuse or disturb
3. deficit   (　　)   **c.** new and expanding
4. disrupt   (　　)   **d.** shortage
5. start-up   (　　)   **e.** knowledge or skill

Summary

次の英文は記事の要約です。下の語群から最も適切な語を１つ選び、（　）内に記入しなさい。

1-08

From architecture to (　　　　　), technological changes are affecting a large range of sectors. While some jobs have (　　　　) so thoroughly that workers have to completely (　　　　　), others have (　　　　) that previously did not exist. Britain is one of Europe's more digitally advanced economies, yet it faces a shortage of (　　　　) skilled workers.

> changed   copywriting   emerged   retrain   sufficiently

英国は、2020年１月31日午後11時、47年間加盟していた EU を離脱し、同年末までの「移行期間」に入った。その直後に新型コロナウイルス感染拡大の問題が起った。しかし、英政府は「Brexit over breathing 呼吸よりブレグジット優先」の姿勢を採り、移行期間終了後の政治、外交、経済、社会に焦点を当てる必要がある。中でも労働市場問題が浮上している。

2016年の国民投票で Brexit が決まったが、EU 内の移民問題が主因の１つとなった。イギリスは賃金も高く、教育、医療等も容易に受けられるので、人気があった。逆に、英国民の方は彼らに仕事を取られたと不満を表した。EU 市民の割合は、英国労働市場７％220万人だった。特に、電子、電機、土木、機械等のエンジニアが２万人以上不足していると言われている。

英国の IT 業界では、就労者のうち20％近くが外国生まれで、そのうちの３分の１が EU 諸国出身者だそうだ。IT 就労者の70％が「イギリスを去るつもり」、その大半が「他の EU 諸国へ行く」と調査の結果が出た。

英政府は、Brexit 後、「経済成長を牽引するデジタルセクターを保護し、強化するため」のデジタル戦略として、①国民400万人のスキル向上② AI とロボット工学研究用に大学に1730万ポンドの助成金③政府と IT 業界との情報交換④大学生に年５億ポンドのローン⑤技術訓練向上などに力を入れると発表している。

Reading

1-09

Building the UK's tech workforce

A shortage of workers with expertise, from search engine optimisation to cloud computing, has created a digital skills gap—and both staff and employers must adapt, write Sylvia Klimaki

TECHNOLOGY is rapidly and fundamentally changing the way most people do their jobs, disrupting the nature of work and increasing the demand for new kinds of digital skills.

1-10

5　The impact can be felt in all kinds of jobs. Gone are the days of copywriters simply writing copy, for instance. Now they also need to be familiar with search engines and social media to know what will make their work more visible online. Architects need to be able to create digital concepts as their

10　clients now often expect to see more than a 2D drawing. Accountants have to keep up with rapid digital advances disrupting their industry such as the growth of online filing.

Byron Nicolaides, CEO of PeopleCert, a professional skills assessment and certification business, says: "The digital

15　skill gap describes the effect that has resulted from a shift towards digitalization, with the emergence of new professions alongside the displacement of other roles that now require continued digital training."

1-11

Demand for people with high-level digital skills is greater

20　than the supply of suitably qualified employees, and the gap is growing. The World Economic Forum estimates that by 2022 emerging technologies will generate 133 million new jobs in placc of the 75 million that will be displaced.

"If the demand for digital expertise is not able to be met

25　by the supply, the resulting deficit in a skilled workplace will not only affect the ability of businesses to shape their own future, but will hinder the economic growth and generate a new reality of [digital] illiteracy," argue Nicolaides.

tech：デジタル技術

expertise：専門知識［技術・技能］

search engine optimisation：検索エンジン最適化《検索エンジンが検索結果を一覧表示する時に、自分のウェブページが上位に来るように、あらかじめ工夫しておくこと》

cloud computing：クラウド・コンピューティング《コンピューティング資源（ソフトウェア、ハードウェアなど）をインターネットなどのネットワークを介して共同利用するシステム》

demand：需要

Gone are the days：《主語が長いことによる倒置；be動詞＋自動詞の過去分詞→完了形》

copy：宣伝文句

familiar with 〜：〜に精通している

visible：目立つ

Architects：建築家

more than 〜：〜だけではない、〜を超える

Accountants：会計士

filing：書類作成

assessment and certification：専門スキルの評価と認定

business：企業・会社

shift towards 〜：〜への転換・移行

World Economic Forum：世界経済フォーラム《経済や政治のリーダーたちが連携し、世界情勢の改善に取り組む国際機関》

met by 〜：〜によって満たされる

shape 〜：〜を具体化する

1-12

30　　The UK is the fifth most digitally advanced nation in Europe (Finland comes top) according to data from the European Union. It is already home to a large number of big tech businesses and the UK has more tech "unicorns" (start-up businesses valued at $1 billion or more) than any other European country.

35　　According to Tech Nation, a UK network focused on accelerating the growth of digital businesses across the country, in 2018 the UK continued to attract tech talent, employing 5 per cent of all high-growth tech workers globally. In Europe this places the UK behind Germany but ahead of Sweden,
40 France, Denmark and the Netherlands.

1-13

　　Despite this encouraging news, the UK is still facing a significant digital skills shortage. A report from the Open University last year highlights the extent of the problem and its impact on UK companies, with nine in 10 organisations
45 admitting to having a shortage of digital skills.

　　Jules Pipe, London's deputy mayor for planning, regeneration and skills, says the capital needs workers with advanced digital skills. "More than half of the capital's start-ups say a lack of highly skilled workers is their main challenge,
50 while emerging industries—such as artificial intelligence and virtual reality—look for the most cutting-edge talent."

　　He points to the Mayor's Digital Talent Programme, which has supported 800 Londoners into digital careers since 2017, and includes a focus on young women and Londoners from a
55 range of backgrounds.

Evening Standard, March 5, 2020

European Union：欧州連合

unicorns：ユニコーン企業《企業価値が10億ドル以上に達した新興企業》

talent：人材

Open University：オープン大学《誰でも入学できる通信制大学、日本の放送大学》

organisations：会社

challenge：課題

virtual reality：仮想現実

cutting-edge：最先端の

Digital Talent Programme：デジタル技術者養成計画

careers：専門的職業

backgrounds：経歴

Exercises

次の１〜５の英文を完成させるために、 a〜dの中から最も適切なものを１つ選びなさい。

1. One of the messages that this article wished to impart is that
    a. the UK has 5 per cent of the world's "unicorn" businesses.
    b. digital illiteracy within companies is unlikely to hinder growth.
    c. the United Kingdom has an oversupply digital skills.
    d. displaced jobs would be replaced by a greater number of tech jobs.

2. The number one country in digital adaptation is
    a. The UK.
    b. Finland.
    c. Sweden.
    d. Denmark.

3. Copywriters need a wider range of skills because companies are looking for
    a. more typewriters for employees.
    b. employees working from home by computer.
    c. individuals familiar with search engines and social media.
    d. older more experienced employees with traditional techniques.

4. Mr Pipe seems to believe that
    a. his city needs more employees with high level tech skills.
    b. his new TV program about A.I. will be very popular.
    c. virtual reality and other emerging industries lack financial capital.
    d. he can become mayor if he pushes high-tech policies.

5. Without the aid of digitalized technology architects would
    a. go out of business.
    b. only offer customers 2D visualizations.
    c. move to different work sectors such as accountancy.
    d. have to rely on online filing.

本文の内容に合致するものに T（True）、合致しないものに F（False）をつけなさい。

(   ) **1.** Technology is changing the skill-sets required in current jobs.

(   ) **2.** The supply of highly skilled workers can easily meet employers' needs.

(   ) **3.** The UK ranks fifth in Europe in the number of tech unicorns within its borders.

(   ) **4.** Architecture is one of the few jobs hardly affected by digital skills.

(   ) **5.** The Mayor's Digital Talent Programme appears to be very successful in assisting candidates to acquire digital tech skill employment.

Vocabulary

次の英文は、読売新聞の The Japan News「えいご工房」に掲載された *Delivery robots to be tested on public road*『宅配ロボの公道実験』の記事の一部です。下の語群から最も適切なものを１つ選び、(   ) 内に記入しなさい。

Autonomous (   ) robots are expected to be tested on public roads during this fiscal year.

The government aims to have such robots in (   ) use during the next fiscal year or later to address the chronic (   ) of workers in the distribution industry.

A public-private council will be formed to identify (   ) issues among other concerns through these trials before the government considers establishing necessary legislation.

The autonomous delivery robot model to be used in the trials has a box-like body with (   ) and can carry cargo weighing up to tens of kilograms. The robot can (   ) parcels to designated locations using Ground Positioning System data among other sources.

In Japan, such robots are expected to be used for short (   ) from the local base of a delivery company to a home or office, dubbed "last-mile delivery" in the transportation industry. Delivering parcels using trucks and other vehicles requires many drivers who often have to carry heavy items onto carts in narrow streets. The government aims to reduce the (   ) on delivery staff through the use of autonomous delivery robots.

burden	deliver	delivery	distances
practical	safety	shortage	wheels

3

- 日本の報道機関、自国の将来に確信が無い
- 「飛び恥」が航空業界に打撃

米国の学校での気候変動を巡る集会にグレタさんも参加し、発言する

Photo: ロイター／アフロ

Before you read

1. What do you think the article will be about?

   この記事は何の話題についてだと思いますか？

2. What do you know about Greta Thunberg?

   グレタ・トゥーンベリについて何か知っていますか？

次の１〜５の語の説明として最も近いものをa〜eから１つ選び、（　）内に記入しなさい。

1. launch 　　（　　）　　a. initiate
2. appall 　　（　　）　　b. except in the case of
3. barring 　　（　　）　　c. lonely
4. forlorn 　　（　　）　　d. sharp rise
5. spike 　　（　　）　　e. shock

Summary

次の英文は記事の要約です。下の語群から最も適切な語を１つ選び、（　　）内に記入しなさい。

1-14

A recent report involving 153 countries (　　　　　) that little has been done to tackle climate change, (　　　　　) 40 years of discussion. Greta Thunberg, and thousands who follow the young Swedish activist, (　　　　　). (　　　　　) airlines are recognizing the need to reduce carbon emissions. But the US president is withdrawing his country from international (　　　　　) programs.

agree　　concludes　　despite　　environmental　　even

2003年１月３日、スウェーデンの首都ストックホルムで、環境活動家の Greta Ernman Thunberg グレタ・エルンマン・トゥーンベリが誕生した。彼女の母親は、著名なオペラ歌手、父親は俳優である。

彼女が８歳のときに、気候変動について知り、落ち込んで無気力になった。その後、アスペルガー症候群、強迫性障害、選択的無言症と診断された。診断から２年後、菜食主義者となり、飛行機には乗らず、彼女の言動に家族の同意を求めた。アスペルガーを病気とみなさず、代わりに「スーパーパワー」と呼び始めた。

そして、グレタが15歳の時に、気候変動に対するストライキとスピーチを学校で開始した。スウェーデン議会前に一人で座り込み、より強い気候変動対策を求める活動を始めた。「Friday for future 未来のための金曜日」という名で、気候変動学校スト運動を組織した。その後、国連の「気候変動サミット」でグレタが演説した後、世界160か国以上で温暖化対策の強化を求める抗議デモが行われた。グレタは、SNSなどで世界の注目を集め、「グレタ・トゥーンベリ効果」と呼ばれ、多くの学生や政治家たちに大きな影響を与えている。COP24などの国際会議に招かれ、演説を行った。温室効果ガスを大量に排出するとして飛行機の利用を避け、サミット出席のために英国からヨットで２週間かけて大西洋を横断した。

Reading

News outlets are uncertain about the nation's future

"How dare you?" demanded Greta Thunberg of world leaders at the U.N. in September. The 16-year-old Swedish climate activist was furious. "All you can talk about," she said, "is money and fairy tales about eternal economic growth."

5　That's all there *is* to talk about, U.S. President Donald Trump in effect replied to her last week, formally launching his country's withdrawal from the green-house-gas-limiting Paris agreement.

The next day, as though in reply to *him*, a global team
10 of 11,258 scientists in 153 countries declared a climate emergency of appalling proportions, foreseeing "untold human suffering," barring vast changes not at present on the horizon. "Despite 40 years of global climate negotiations, with few exceptions, we have generally conducted business
15 as usual and have largely failed to address this predicament," the report said.

Thunberg's activism began in August 2018 with lonely sit-ins in front of the Swedish parliament. Her placard read, "Schools strike for climate." She cut a forlorn figure. Did
20 she foresee then the global movement she now leads? "The movement's momentum has even reached Japan," Metropolis magazine observed acidly this past August. Fridays for Future Tokyo held its first rally in February—"its 20 or so student protesters outnumbered by reporters." Organizers persisted
25 and the numbers rose—to thousands at best, compared to tens of thousands elsewhere in the world.

"I wanted to change people's awareness like Greta, but I couldn't," organizer Sayaka Miyazaki, a 22-year-old Rikkyo University student, lamented to the Asahi Shimbun in
30 September.

She may yet. Greta didn't become Greta overnight.

The Japan Times, November 17, 2019

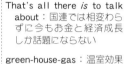

News outlets：報道機関

That's all there *is* to talk about：国連では相変わらずに今もお金と経済成長しか話題にならない

green-house-gas：温室効果ガス《温室効果の原因となる気体；一酸化炭素、二酸化炭素、フロン、メタンなど》

Paris agreement：パリ協定

appalling proportions：最悪の比率であること

on the horizon：近い将来の

address 〜：〜に取り組む、対処する

activism：積極的行動

lonely sit-ins：一人での座り込み抗議

cut a forlorn figure：孤独で寂しそうに見えた

Metropolis：メトロポリス《東京に在住する英語を話す外国人を対象とする無料の月刊雑誌》

Fridays for Future Tokyo：「未来のための金曜日東京・グローバル気候マーチ」日本で主催する団体

student protesters：学生から成るデモ参加者

awareness：意識

yet：いつか

'Flight-shaming' could slow growth of airline industry, says IATA

35

| Climate now 'top of the agenda' for investors as airlines try to lower carbon emissions |

Escalating pressure from investors is pushing airlines to address environmental concerns, according to the International Air Transport Association (IATA), which acknowledged that the trend toward "flight-shaming" could weigh on the
40 industry's future growth.

Speaking at a conference in London where airlines vied to demonstrate plans to decarbonise, IATA said the climate was now "top of the agenda" for investors.

Citing HSBC research, IATA's chief economist, Brian
45 Pearce, said climate issues came up an average of seven times on each call between European airlines and investors in 2019, compared with an average of less than once per earnings call between 2013 and 2017.

Pearce said: "Climate change is not just an issue for
50 protestors or scientists. You can see the spike this year. This is on the top of the agenda for mainstream investors now. We're getting pressure from all quarters."

He said *flygskam*, or flight-shaming—the trend towards making air travel socially unacceptable due to its carbon cost
55 — "could be a factor slowing growth in the future."

Although airlines have signed up to Corsia offsetting scheme set up by the UN aviation agency, ICAO, many believe taxes and a consumer backlash could grow. Shai Weiss, Virgin Atlantic's chief executive, said: "If there is one
60 name everyone in the airline industry knows today that it perhaps didn't know a year ago, it's Greta Thunberg."

The Guardian, October 17, 2019

Flight-shaming：飛び恥

IATA：国際航空運送協会

top of the agenda：第一検討事項

carbon emissions：炭素排出量

environmental concerns：環境問題

weigh on 〜：〜を圧迫する

vied to 〜：争って〜した

decarbonise：化石燃料依存から脱却する、脱炭素化する

HSBC：香港上海銀行《ロンドンに本社を置く世界的な金融持株会社》

came up on 〜：〜に出た

call：コールオプション《指定期間内の指定価格での「買い付け」》

earnings call：（投資家向けの）収支報告、業績発表

due to its carbon cost：炭素排出という代償のせいで

Corsia：国際航空のための炭素相殺計画

ICAO：国際民間航空機関

consumer backlash：消費者からの反発

Virgin Atlantic：ヴァージン・アトランティック航空《大陸間の長距離国際線をメインに運航する英国の航空会社》

Exercises

次の1〜5の英文を完成させるために、a〜dの中から最も適切なものを1つ選びなさい。

1. Greta Thunberg feels that

    a. the world must seriously deal with climate change.
    b. the world is seriously dealing with the problem of climate change.
    c. governments need to focus more on economic growth.
    d. President Trump has not focused enough on economic growth.

2. Sayaka Miyazaki has expressed her feelings of

    a. happiness about the success of ecological movements.
    b. boredom with talking to citizens about the future.
    c. disappointment at being unable to persuade more people.
    d. sadness over Greta Thunberg's recent inactivity.

3. One thing that airlines fear may reduce their profits in future is

    a. the rising price of fuel.
    b. the environmental cost of carbon.
    c. lower taxes on passengers.
    d. lower support for Thunberg.

4. Investors are becoming more interested in

    a. financial profits and losses.
    b. environmental repercussions from flying.
    c. the financial benefits of higher taxes.
    d. the dangers of decarbonizing flights.

5. The word "flygskam" refers to

    a. airline travel becoming socially unacceptable.
    b. the low effect of carbon on our environment.
    c. consumers' rising demand for flights.
    d. all of the above statements.

本文の内容に合致するものに T（True）、合致しないものに F（False）をつけなさい。

(   ) **1.** People will probably be flying more often with reduced airline ticket prices.

(   ) **2.** Greta Thunberg spoke to the U.N. and reprimanded them for not focusing on climate change.

(   ) **3.** A report says that environmental changes have been ignored for more than 60 years.

(   ) **4.** Greta Thunberg made a huge impact on the world, including investors.

(   ) **5.** When Greta first started fighting to make people aware of climate change, she was not a popular speaker.

Vocabulary

次の英文は、the Japan Times に掲載された *Greta Thunberg and German railway engage in raging 'tweetstorm'*『グレタ・トゥーンベリとドイツ鉄道会社が荒れ狂ったツイートストームに取り組む』の記事の一部です。下の語群から最も適切なものを１つ選び、（   ）内に記入しなさい。

Climate activist Greta Thunberg and Germany's national railway company created a tweetstorm Sunday after she (   ) a photo of herself sitting on the (   ) of a train surrounded by lots of bags. The image has drawn plenty of comment online about the performance of German railways. Thunberg posted the tweet late Saturday with the comment "traveling on overcrowded (   ) through Germany. And I'm finally on my way home!"

But German railway company suggested that Thunberg may not have spent the whole time sitting on the floor. And the 16-year-old Swedish activist later sought to draw a line under the matter by tweeting that she eventually got a (   ) and that overcrowded trains are a good thing. Some Twitter users expressed (   ) for Thunberg for not being able to get a proper seat on the train for the long ride home from Madrid, where she was attending months of traveling by trains and (   ) to different climate events in Europe and the United States.

Thunberg doesn't fly on planes because it's considered (   ) to the climate. Last week, she was named Time magazine's Person of the Year for her efforts to (   ) government and others to take faster actions in fighting climate change.

boats	floor	harmful	pity
posted	prod	seat	trains

●コアラが森林火災の犠牲に

オーストラリア東部の山火事でコアラ病院に保護され、手当てを受ける絶滅危惧種のコアラ

Photo: Splash ／アフロ

Before you read

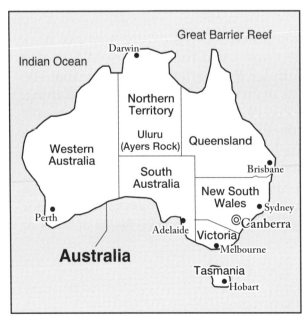

Commonwealth of Australia
オーストラリア 連邦
英連邦王国の一国

面積　7,692,024km²（日本の約20倍）（世界６位）
人口　24,990,000人（世界55位）
民族　ヨーロッパ系　80%
　　　アジア系　12%　／アボリジニ　2％
首都　キャンベラ
最大都市　シドニー
公用語　英語
宗教　キリスト教　52%
　　　（カトリック　25.8%　／聖公会　18.7%）
　　　非キリスト教　5％　／無宗教　30%
識字率　99%
政体　立憲君主制
GDP　1兆3,379億米ドル（世界14位）
　　　1人当たり GDP　55,707米ドル（世界11位）
通貨　オーストラリア・ドル

次の１〜５の語の説明として最も近いものをa〜eから１つ選び、（　）内に記入しなさい。

1. plight 　　　　（　　）　　　a. thoroughly burn
2. singe 　　　　（　　）　　　b. wrap in cloth
3. swaddle 　　　（　　）　　　c. bad situation
4. incinerate 　　（　　）　　　d. psychological pain
5. distress 　　　（　　）　　　e. partly burn

Summary

次の英文は記事の要約です。下の語群から最も適切な語を１つ選び、（　　）内に記入しなさい。

1-20

　Koalas are among the worst (　　　　　　) of terrible fires that have destroyed millions of (　　　　　) of Australian forest. Fires are (　　　　　) in Australia, and although koalas do not run away like kangaroos or snakes, they do have some defense (　　　　　). But the intensity of recent conflagrations has been too much for a (　　　　) that is already endangered.

acres　　common　　species　　strategies　　victims

　オーストラリアには、コアラが４万匹から８万匹いるとされるが、個体数が減少し、International Union for Conservation of Nature 国際自然保護連合は、絶滅の危険のある「危急種」に指定している。コアラの生息数減に歯止めをかけるため、2018年にはニューサウスウエールズ州の森林地帯を保護区や国立公園に指定する「コアラ戦略」を発表している。
　しかし、2019年９月以降、東部ニューサウスウエールズ州では、270万ヘクタール以上の森林が焼失し、720棟以上の建物が被害を受けた。温暖化や気候変動により降雨不足のため火災が拡大したのが要因とされる。12月には、オーストラリアSBS放送が、森林火災で2000匹以上のコアラが死んだのではないかと報じた。
　2019年11月下旬までにブラジル国内で起きた森林火災は、18万件を超え、その６割以上がアマゾン川岸に集中した。野焼きの火の延焼が一因だと言われている。１年間に違法伐採や火災などで失われたアマゾンの森林面積は、日本の青森県に匹敵すると言われている。世界の環境保護団体は、アマゾンを「地球の肺」と訴えている。アマゾンの土はやせているため、牧草や農作物の育ちが悪い。農業や牛を飼っている人たちは、肥料が買えずに、代わりに灰を得るため開墾後も野焼きを繰り返している。

Reading

1-21

Saving the Fire Victims Who Cannot Flee: Australia's Koalas

> The plight of dozens of animals being treated for burned paws and singed fur is raising fears about climate change and the future of the species.

MELBOURNE, Australia — The victims were carried in one by one, their paws burned and fur singed, suffering from dehydration and fear. Their caretakers bandaged their wounds, swaddled them and laid them in baskets with the
5　only thing that was familiar — the leaves of a eucalyptus tree.

1-22

As catastrophic fires have burned more than two million acres in Australia, dozens of koalas have been rescued from smoldering trees and ashen ground. The animals, already threatened as a species before these latest blazes ravaged a
10　crucial habitat, are being treated in rescue centers, and at least one private home, along the country's east coast.

"They are terrified," said Cheyne Flanagan, the clinical director of the Koala Hospital, in Port Macquarie, the only facility of its kind in the world. She added that what was
15　happening to the koalas was "a national tragedy."

Officials at the hospital began warning weeks ago, when the fires first ignited around Port Macquarie, 250 miles north of Sydney, that hundreds of koalas may have been "incinerated."

The plight of the koala — a national symbol of Australia
20　— has raised questions among conservationists and scientists about what it will take to preserve biodiversity in a country increasingly prone to intense fire, extreme heat and water scarcity, and which already has among the highest rates of species extinction in the world.

25　While koalas have evolved to exist alongside wildfires, the animals are facing new threats not just from climate change but also from human development, which has dislocated local populations, impairing their ability to survive fires. In some

Flee：逃げる

plight：窮状
paws：手足
species：種（としてのコアラ）

dehydration：脱水症

swaddled ～：～を布で包んだ

acres：エーカー《1エーカーは約4,000m²》

ravaged ～：～を荒廃させた
habitat：生息環境

clinical director：臨床部長・院長

warning ～：～と警報を発する《目的語は that 以下》
incinerated：焼却処分される
conservationists：環境保護活動家
biodiversity：生物多種多様性
prone to ～：～の傾向がある
which already has among the highest rates of species extinction：オーストラリアは既に絶滅種の比率が最も高い国だ《have among ～は be among ～の変形》
exist alongside ～：～と共存する
dislocated local populations：地元住民を立ち退かせた《コアラを指す》
impairing ～：～を弱める

regions, scientists say, koalas' numbers have declined by up
30 to 80 percent, though it is difficult to know how many remain
across Australia.

1-24

"We have these unique animals not found anywhere else
on this planet, and we're killing them," Ms. Flanagan said.
"This is a big wake-up call."

35 The animal distress goes beyond koalas. Recently, tens of
thousands of bats plummeted from the sky in temperatures
exceeding 107 degrees Fahrenheit in northern Australia.
Kangaroos, parched by drought, decimated the grapes on
a vineyard in Canberra. And waterfowl in the Macquarie
40 Marshes, a wildlife haven in northwest New South Wales,
have been affected by a fire in their habitat.

1-25

Koalas, unlike kangaroos, birds or snakes, do not flee from
fires, but instead scale trees to the canopy, where they can curl
themselves into a ball for protection and wait for the danger to
45 pass.

But during high-intensity fires, such as those that have
burned in recent weeks, the animals, conservationists say,
are far less likely to survive. Even if the fire itself does not
reach the tree canopy, the animals may overheat and fall to the
50 ground, where they can be burned to death.

The New York Times, November 14, 2019

---

by up to 〜：最高〜ほど
《by は程度を表す》

wake-up call：警鐘

plummeted：まっすぐに落
ちた

Fahrenheit：（温度を示す）
華氏《(F−32)×$\frac{5}{9}$＝C》
107F＝42C

parched by drought：干ば
つで喉がからからに乾いて

decimated 〜：〜を台無し
にした

Macquarie Marshes：マッ
コーリー湿地

wildlife haven：野生生物
保護区

canopy：樹冠

far less likely to 〜：ほと
んど〜しそうにない

Exercises

Multiple Choice

次の１〜３の英文の質問に答え、４〜５の英文を完成させるために、 a 〜 d の中から最も適切なものを１つ選びなさい。

1. Most animals flee fires, but which do not depart at the first sign?

    a. Kangaroos.

    b. Snakes.

    c. Koalas.

    d. Orangutans.

2. What percentage of koalas have disappeared from Australia?

    a. 8%.   **c.** 48%.

    b. 18%.   **d.** 80%.

3. What item were injured koalas bandaged in and comforted by?

    a. Eucalyptus leaves.

    b. Baskets.

    c. Rescuers.

    d. Fur.

4. The many massive fires in Australia are an indication of

    a. overcrowding in the cities.

    b. tree-cutting throughout the country.

    c. bats invading the woods.

    d. climate change affecting the country.

5. The koala is described as

    a. unable to eat grapes.

    b. a national symbol.

    c. able to deal with fires.

    d. all of the above.

本文の内容に合致するものにT（True）、合致しないものにF（False）をつけなさい。

(   )   **1.** Scientists believe that in high intensity fires animals are likely to not survive.

(   )   **2.** Growth in Australia's human development is relevant to the displacement of koalas.

(   )   **3.** Many citizens of Australia are concerned about the future of koalas.

(   )   **4.** Koalas are native to several other countries.

(   )   **5.** Australia already has the highest level of species extinction.

Vocabulary

次の英文は、the Japan Times に掲載された *Coronavirus outbreak's silver lining for climate crisis likely to fade*『コロナウイルス発生は、薄れて行きそうな気候変動危機への明るい見通しだ』の記事の一部です。下の語群から最も適切なものを１つ選び、(   ) 内に記入しなさい。

Economic shock waves from the coronavirus outbreak have curbed (   ) pollution from China and beyond, but hopes for (   ) benefits from the slowdown are likely to be dashed quickly, experts say.

As governments prepare to spend their way out of the crisis, including with large infrastructure projects, global (   ) concerns will be little more than an afterthought, dwarfed by a drive to (   ) up a stuttering world economy, they say.

In the four weeks up to March 1, China's discharge of carbon dioxide (   ) 200 million tons, or 25 percent, compared to the same period last year, according to the Center for Research on Energy and Clean Air (CREA)- (   ) to annual carbon dioxide emissions from Argentina, Egypt or Vietnam.

As the country's economy (   ) to a crawl, coal consumption at power plants in China declined by 36 percent, and the use of oil at refineries by nearly as much.

"When you turn off the global fossil fuel economy, greenhouse gas emissions go down, air quality (   )," said Jon Erickson. But any climate silver lining will be short-lived, experts warn.

carbon	climate	equivalent	fell
improves	prop	slowed	warming

上流階級育ちの坊ちゃんの中身のない自信に気をつけろ

英国オックスフォード大学での卒業式後の新卒業生たち。出身高校によって進むべき
将来が異なるのか？　　　　　　　　　　　　　　　Photo: ロイター／アフロ

Before you read

1. What do you think the article will be about?

   この記事は何の話題についてだと思いますか？

2. What do you know about posh boys?

   上流階級育ちの坊ちゃんについて何か知っていますか？

次の１〜５の語の説明として最も近いものを a 〜 e から１つ選び、（　）内に記入しなさい。

1. hollow	（　　）	**a.**	insistence
2. assertiveness	（　　）	**b.**	empty or baseless
3. slickness	（　　）	**c.**	run away
4. scurry	（　　）	**d.**	brutal honesty
5. bluntness	（　　）	**e.**	superficial confidence

Summary

次の英文は記事の要約です。下の語群から最も適切な語を１つ選び、（　　）内に記入しなさい。

1-26

The economic and political dominance of the privately-educated (　　　　　　) in Britain. Even if they have only average intelligence, their confidence and social (　　　　　　) bring them huge advantages. Overconfidence is known to be a (　　　　　　) of errors and failures. But an expensive education and posh (　　　　　　) still give these people (　　　　　　) influence over politics, law and banking.

accent   connections   disproportionate   persists   source

　　18世紀後半に誕生したイギリスの階級は、産業革命の中から生まれた社会構造の変革だった。Upper Class 上流階級、Middle Class 中流階級、Working Class 労働者階級の３階級に分かれている。その後、中流階級にも upper middle class 上位中流階級、middle middle class 中位中流階級、lower middle class 下位中流階級に細分化され、５つの階級に分かれている。中には、７つの階級に分類する学者もいる。上流階級は、王族・貴族で構成され、上位中流階級は、医師、弁護士、官僚、軍人、中位中流が国会議員、企業経営者、会社重役、新聞記者、教師、警部、下位中流階級に不動産屋、写真家、銀行員、秘書、警官に当てはめることができる。労働者階級は、バスの運転手、土木作業員、日雇い労働者などの肉体労働者をさす。

　　現代のイギリスには、法的に制度化された階級はないが、人々の生活や意識の中に階級社会はしっかりと存在している。階級間には積極的な交流はなく、学校、購読新聞、使う英語の単語・アクセントなどが違う。所得や貯蓄、住宅資産などの経済、社会的紐帯の数と状況などの社会関係、美術館やコンサートへ行くなどの高尚な文化が階級格差を示している。上位中流階級は、社会的ネットワークに恵まれている。

Reading

1-27

Beware the posh boy's hollow self-confidence

We can't improve social mobility until we stop trusting in a firm handshake and cut-glass accent

    Sixty years ago at Cambridge, Alan Bennet encountered public school boys for the first time. "I was appalled," he remembered, "they were loud, self-confident and all seemed to know one another." In 2011, at Oxford, I had the same
5 reaction. This time they were all wearing tracksuits but the extraordinary levels of self-confidence were just as Bennet had recorded. Nothing had changed.

1-28

    A study reported in *The Times* yesterday proves the bleedin' obvious; poshness breeds confidence. The higher
10 your perception of your social class, the more confident you're likely to be. Depressingly, the researchers then showed that confidence is an indicator of success, which in turn is an indicator of high social class, which is an indicator of confidence. You get the picture; it's a vicious circle.

15   A 2016 report by the Sutton Trust found that sociability, confidence and assertiveness are "particularly beneficial for career success". People with those traits are 25 per cent more likely to be in jobs that pay more than £40,000 a year. The same study found that those characteristics were overwhelmingly
20 associated with people from affluent backgrounds. And not only will a private education land you a better paying job, it'll land you a more powerful job too. The privately educated are disproportionately represented in roles with greater opportunities for decision-making and leadership.

1-29

25   When you pay £30,000 a year to send your child to private school you're mainly buying confidence. You get good grades, sure (about 50 per cent of privately educated kids get As and A*s at A level), but the confidence takes you even further. A privately educated man leaving university with the same
30 degree as a state-educated man will go on to earn 7 to 15 per

---

posh：上流階級育ちの
hollow：中身のない

social mobility：社会的流動性

cut-glass accent：上流階級のような発音

public school：パブリックスクール《英国では中高一貫の私立学校》

The Times：タイムズ《英国で1785年に創刊された世界最古の日刊新聞；政治的傾向は中道右派》

bleedin' obvious：非常に明白なこと《ロンドン下町言葉》

You get the picture：話が見えただろう

vicious circle：悪循環

Sutton Trust：サットントラスト《英国の教育慈善団体》

assertiveness：自己主張

traits：特徴・特質

from affluent backgrounds：裕福な環境で育った

private education：（小中高の）私教育《公教育はstate education》

land ～ …：～を…に連れていく

powerful job：力をふるえる仕事

As and A*s at A level：大学入試資格を得るAレベルでの（成績の）優(A)や秀(S)

cent more.

1-30

In the five years since I left university I've observed this phenomenon myself. My privately educated contemporaries are much more likely to be working in high-status careers 35 like law, banking or journalism. Many of my state-educated friends work in service jobs or have moved back to their home towns. I'm sure the lack of confidence to have a go in highly competitive industries is a factor.

As a country we're as awed by posh confidence as we've ever 40 been; the slickness of the hair, the firmness of the handshake. A glance at our political leaders confirms this. The sackings and political disasters endured by Boris Johnson might have sent a less assertive man scurrying back to his burrow. Not so Boris; his ironclad Etonian confidence is propelling him 45 towards the leadership of the Conservative Party.

1-31

If posh confidence isn't going away, it's up to us to wean ourselves off the habit of equating confidence with ability. After all, the consequences could be terrible. The researchers from the first study I quoted point out with engaging bluntness 50 that "overconfidence is believed to be a significant underlying cause for many catastrophes, such as wars, strikes, litigation, entrepreneurial failures, and stock market bubbles". And you thought Boris Johnson was bad.

The Times, May 22, 2019

confirm 〜：〜を裏付ける

Boris Johnson：ボリス・ジョンソン英国現首相

burrow：隠れ穴、避難場所

Etonian：イートン校卒業生の《英国の超名門パブリックスクール》

propelling 〜 towards …：〜を…へ駆り立てる

Conservative Party：保守党《英国２大政党の１つ》

up to us：私たち次第だ

wean ourselves off 〜：〜を止める

equating 〜 with …：〜と…を同一視する

with engaging bluntness：ひときわ目立つほどの無愛想さで

underlying cause：根本原因

litigation：訴訟

entrepreneurial：起（企）業家の

stock market：証券市場

And you thought 〜：さあ、これで〜と思っただろう

Exercises

次の１〜５の英文を完成させるために、ａ〜ｄの中から最も適切なものを１つ選びなさい。

1. This article states that

    a. those from public schools will earn 7 to 15% less than students from state schools.

    b. those from a state school will earn 7 to 15% more than the public school students.

    c. confidence acquired from the home and public school environment may enable students to raise their salary earning power.

    d. there is little relationship between the kind of schooling received and confidence and success in the business world.

2. The qualities attributed to "posh boys" include

    a. sociability.

    b. assertiveness.

    c. confidence.

    d. all of the above.

3. By "vicious circle", the author means that

    a. public school students have qualities necessary for success reinforced by their affluent family, teachers, and fellow students.

    b. intelligence, rather than schooling, affects one's job and salary.

    c. Boris Johnson lacks the proper credentials to be a "posh boy."

    d. confidence and sociability are less important in today's world.

4. Overconfidence can have negative consequences such as

    a. business success.

    b. exceptional ability.

    c. economic problems.

    d. lack of ambition.

5. The author of this article feels

    a. Johnson is capable but lacks confidence.

    b. poshness has become a barrier to becoming prime minister.

    c. we need to stop trusting in the abilities of the posh.

    d. we are fortunate to have politicians from elite backgrounds.

本文の内容に合致するものにＴ（True）、合致しないものにＦ（False）をつけなさい。

(   ) **1.** High social class seems to be determined by family background, the school attended, and the personality traits acquired.

(   ) **2.** Jobs worked by state school graduates tend to be lower paying and less valued.

(   ) **3.** A firm handshake has little influence on employment success.

(   ) **4.** You would probably find more lawyers attended public schools.

(   ) **5.** According to this article in certain situations tracksuits are seemingly worn by public school students.

Vocabulary

次の１～６は、「posh」を使用している英文です。下の語群から１つ選び、(   )
内に記入しなさい。

1. She celebrated her birthday at the (   ) hotel in town.

2. She talks so (   ) she sounds like the Queen.

3. She will be getting all (   ) up for a banquet.

4. She is thinking of (   ) up her apartment with new curtains.

5. She drives a Rolls-Royce? You can't get (   ) than that.

6. (   ) has become a path to promotion.

posh	poshed	posher
poshest	poshing	poshness

Unit **6**

●超人間的な AI は御免だ

ドイツのルフトハンザ航空がミュンヘン空港での案内係として、人型ロボット
「ペッパー」を導入　　　　　　　　　　　　　　Photo: picture alliance ／アフロ

Before you read

1. What do you think the article will be about?

   この記事は何の話題についてだと思いますか？

2. How useful do you think A.I. is?

   AI がどのように役立つと思いますか？

Words and Phrases

次の1〜5の語の説明として最も近いものをa〜eから1つ選び、(　)内に記入しなさい。

1. preoccupy　　　(　　)　　**a.** intended to prevent in advance
2. beneficial　　　(　　)　　**b.** captivate or obsess
3. confine　　　　(　　)　　**c.** useful
4. preemptive　　 (　　)　　**d.** very important
5. crucial　　　　(　　)　　**e.** limit

Summary

次の英文は記事の要約です。下の語群から最も適切な語を1つ選び、(　)内に記入しなさい。

1-32

The biggest danger humans (　　　　　) from A.I. is its superior ability to anticipate. Having no goals of their own, machines are (　　　　　) to achieve the objectives that humans give them. But highly intelligent machines may come up with (　　　　　) that humans never expected. Unless we are (　　　　　) of this, their activities may end up (　　　　　) us.

| aware | face | harming | programmed | solutions |

　AI (Artificial Intelligence) 人工知能は、自動運転車、Deep Learning 深層学習、SIRI 秘書機能アプリ、UCAV 無人戦闘機、自律型ロボット兵器、検索 algorithm アルゴリズム、顔認証に至るまで急速な進歩を遂げて来ている。Deep Learning 深層学習は最新の人工知能理論を導入している。その技術は、囲碁・将棋、入試受験、医療の画像診断、車の自動運転、株式投資、小説や芸術などの分野にも応用されている。

　現在使われている AI は、狭義の人工知能つまり弱い AI で、特定な作業が行われるように設計されている。人間が全認知能力を必要としない程度の問題解決や推論を行うソフトウエアの研究を指し、知能を感じさせることのない特定問題解決器でしかないのである。

　一方、広義の人工知能つまり強い AI は、多くの研究者の長期的な目標となっている。人間の知能に迫るようになるか、人間の仕事をこなせるようになるか、幅広い知識と何らかの自意識を持つようになったときに強い AI と呼ばれるようになるのではないか。これらには、人間と同様の感性や思考回路を持つ「汎用人工知能」、人間が意図的に作成する知的物を真であると提案する「合成知能」、技術で作成された人工物に意識を持たせる「人工意識」等が挙げられる。

　現在開発されている AI のほとんどは問題特化型で、1つのモデル化・数学化した問題の解決にのみ機能していると言われている。

Reading

1-33

Stopping superhuman A.I.

The arrival of superhuman machine intelligence will be the biggest event in human history. The world's great powers are finally waking up to this fact, and the world's largest corporations have known it for some time. But what they may
5 not fully understand is that *how* A.I. evolves will determine whether this event is also our last.

The problem is not the science-fiction plot that preoccupies Hollywood and the media—the humanoid robot that spontaneously becomes conscious and decides to hate
10 humans. Rather, it is the creation of machines that can draw on more information and look further into the future than humans can, exceeding our capacity for decision making in the real world.

1-34

The "standard model" in A.I., borrowed from philosophical
15 and economic notions of rational behavior, looks like this:

"Machines are intelligent to the extent that their actions can be expected to achieve their objectives."

Because machines, unlike humans, have no objectives of their own, we give them objectives to achieve. In other
20 words, we build machines, feed objectives into them, and off they go. The more intelligent the machine, the more likely it is to complete that objective.

1-35

Unfortunately, this standard model is a mistake. It makes no sense to design machines that are beneficial to us *only if* we
25 write down our objectives completely and correctly, because if we insert the wrong objective into the machine and it is more intelligent than us, we lose.

Until recently, we avoided the potentially serious consequences of poorly designed objectives only because our
30 A.I. technology was not especially smart and it was mostly confined to the lab.

1-36

The effects of a superintelligent algorithm operating on a

great powers：大国、列強

corporations：法人、民間企業

last：最も望ましくない出来事（one の省略）

preoccupies ～：～を夢中にさせる

becomes conscious：意識を持つようになる

it is ～ that …：《強調構文》

notions of ～：～の概念

to the extent that ～：～の程度まで

objectives：目的

off they go：始める《倒置による強調》

complete ～：～を達成する

makes no sense：意味をなさない

only if ～：～の場合に限り

only because ～：～だからといってそれだけで

effects of ～ on …：～の…に及ぼす影響

algorithm：演算アルゴリズム《アルゴリズムとは数学的な問題を解くための一連の手順》

global scale could be far more severe. What if a superintelligent climate control system, given the job of restoring carbon
35 dioxide concentrations to preindustrial levels, believes the solution is to reduce the human population to zero?

　　Some A.I. researchers like to claim that "we can always just switch them off"— but this makes no more sense than arguing that we can always just play better moves than the
40 superhuman chess or Go program we're facing. The machine will anticipate all the ways in which a human might interfere and take preemptive steps to prevent this from happening.

1-37

　　The solution, then, is to change the way we think about A.I. Instead of building machines that exist to achieve *their*
45 objectives, we want a model that looks like this:

　　"Machines are beneficial to the extent that their actions can be expected to achieve our objectives."

　　This fix might seem small, but it is crucial. Machines that have *our* objective as their only guiding principle will
50 be necessarily *uncertain* about what these objectives are, because they are in us—all eight billion of us, in all our glorious variety, and in generations yet unborn—not in the machine.

The New York Times, October 11, 2019

---

global scale：全世界

What if 〜 ?：もし〜としたらどうなるだろうか

climate control：気候変動対策

restoring 〜 to …：〜を…に戻す
concentrations：濃度

preindustrial：産業革命前の

makes no more sense than 〜：〜と同様に意味がない

moves：指し手

preemptive steps：予防措置

fix 〜：〜を調整する

crucial：極めて重大な

guiding principle：指針、行動規範

they are in us：目的は私たち人間が抱く目的

glorious variety：壮大な多様性

Exercises

Multiple Choice

次の1～5の英文を完成させるために、a～dの中から最も適切なものを1つ選びなさい。

1. One problem with super human machine intelligence is

   a. robot hatred for human beings.

   b. intelligent robots' ability to look further into the future than humans can.

   c. humans who lack objectives.

   d. Artificial Intelligence understanding abstract concepts.

2. The standard model is a mistake because

   a. we could insert the incorrect objectives.

   b. we keep developing A.I. in labs and not in practical settings.

   c. robots may go beyond how we thought.

   d. all of the above are true.

3. One disastrous scenario suggested in the article is

   a. climate control systems reducing carbon dioxide by decreasing the human population.

   b. humans trying to turn off machines too soon.

   c. machines' failure to anticipate human reactions.

   d. inserting the wrong objective into a new program.

4. The problematic carbon "solution" seems to be a consequence of

   a. machines telling us what our objectives are.

   b. machines only having the objectives we give them.

   c. scientists producing robots that are too human.

   d. scientists designing robots with poor analytical skills.

5. The author argues for the need for machines that

   a. anticipate human reactions faster.

   b. turn themselves off whenever there is a problem.

   c. are clearer about their own objectives.

   d. understand the complexity of human objectives better.

本文の内容に合致するものに T（True）、合致しないものに F（False）をつけなさい。

(   ) **1.** Super human machine intelligence is described as of unprecedented importance.

(   ) **2.** The title "Stopping Superhuman A.I." leads one to believe that A.I. is slowing down.

(   ) **3.** Machines have objectives of their own.

(   ) **4.** The key contrast in the two quotes given is between "their" and "our."

(   ) **5.** We are now in the final phase of solving the problems associated with A.I.

Vocabulary

次の１〜８は、AI（Artificial Intelligence）に関する語句です。下のa〜hの説明文の中から最も適切なものを１つ選び、（   ）内に記入しなさい。

1. app   (   )
2. AlphaGo   (   )
3. AI   (   )
4. Smartphone   (   )
5. Tablet   (   )
6. SIRI   (   )
7. UCAV   (   )
8. drone   (   )

a. a mobile phone that can be used as a small computer connected to the internet

b. a shortening of the term "application software"

c. a personal mobile computer which is used by tapping with a finger on a touch screen

d. the first computer program to defeat a professional human GO player

e. a virtual assistant operating voice queries and a natural language user interface

f. the ability of a computer program to think and learn, and also a field of study which tries to make computers smart

g. an unmanned combat aerial vehicle and also known as a combat drone

h. an aircraft without a pilot that is controlled by someone on the ground

● ノート型パソコンのリサイクルでの代償：タイで有毒ガスが

タイ国内の電子廃棄物処理工場で作業する外国人労働者
Photo: The New York Times ／ Redux ／ **アフロ**

Before you read

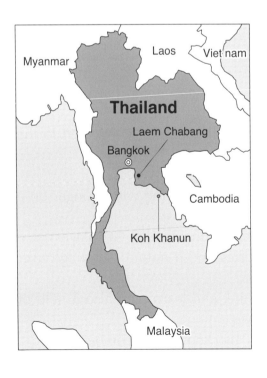

Kingdom of Thailand
タイ王国
面積　514,000km²（日本の約1.4倍）（世界50位）
人口　68,910,000人（世界20位）
公用語　タイ語
首都　バンコク
民族　タイ族　75％
　　　華人　14％
　　　マレー系、インド系、モン族、カレン族
宗教　仏教　94％
　　　イスラム教　5％
GDP　4,872億ドル（世界26位）
　　　1人当たり GDP　7,187ドル（世界84位）
通貨　バーツ
政体　立憲君主制
識字率　95％

次の１〜５の語の説明として最も近いものを a 〜 e から１つ選び、（　　）内に記入しなさい。

1. crouch	（　）	**a.**	rebuff
2. repel	（　）	**b.**	material from used computers or phones
3. salvage	（　）	**c.**	sit or bend down close to the ground
4. e-waste	（　）	**d.**	well-intentioned
5. virtuous	（　）	**e.**	collect for recycling

Summary

次の英文は記事の要約です。下の語群から最も適切な語を１つ選び、（　　）内に記入しなさい。

1-38

（　　　　　　　　）e-waste seems like a good idea. But it is dirty and (　　　　　　　) dangerous. Conscious of the (　　　　　　　), China and Thailand stopped importing used computers and phones. But the work still goes on in the latter, sometimes (　　　　　　　). One Chinese firm employs low-paid laborers there, many of them (　　　　　　　), to do this hazardous work with little protection.

illegal   potentially   recycling   risks   secretly

1989年に有害廃棄物の国際的な移動を規制する「バーゼル条約」が採択された。さらに、2021年から汚れたプラスティックごみが対象に加わることが決まった。

タイの経済も堅調に推移し、工業化や都市化が進む反面、環境公害問題が引き起こされている。有害廃棄物である廃有機溶剤の適正処理が課題となり、タイ政府の環境セクターが改善に積極的に取り組んでいる。

しかし、2020年３月に新型コロナウイルスの感染防止対策として「非常事態」が宣言され、飲食店は、持ち帰りと宅配での営業のみとなり、プラスティック製の容器、スプーン等が多用され、１日当たりのプラスティックごみ発生量が想定より約15％も増加したと言われている。タイを含む東南アジアは、屋台文化が浸透していて、使い捨てプラスティック製品の大量消費地とされている。ASEAN の「バンコク宣言」が採択され、レジ袋の利用制限が行われている。

日本でもごみ減量のため、reduce 発生抑制、reuse 再使用、recycle 再生利用の３Ｒの推進運動が行われている。2017年末に中国がプラスティックゴミ輸入を禁止したが、スウェーデンでは1904年以来115年以上も年間80万トンのゴミを近隣諸国から輸入している。自国のゴミも含めて埋め立て処理されるのはたった１％、残りの99％中半分がリサイクル、半分は焼却され、電力に転換されている。

1-39

The Price of Recycling Old Laptops: Toxic Fumes in Thailand's Lungs

Price：代償
Laptops：ノート型パソコン
Toxic Fumes：有毒ガス

KOH KHANUN, Thailand — Crouched on the ground in a dimly lit factory, the women picked through the discarded innards of the modern world: batteries, circuit boards and bundles of wires.

KOH KHANUN：カヌン島

picked through ～：～を丹念に調べた

discarded：捨てられた

circuit boards：回路基板

5 They broke down the scrap — known as e-waste — with hammers and raw hands. Men, some with faces wrapped in rags to repel the fumes, shoveled the refuse into a clanking machine that salvages usable metal.

e-waste：電子廃棄物

refuse：廃物、ごみ

1-40

As they toiled, smoke spewed over nearby villages and
10 farms. Residents have no idea what is in the smoke: plastic, metal, who knows? All they know is that it stinks and they feel sick.

spewed over ～：～の上に向かって吐き出た

stinks：悪臭を放つ

The factory, New Sky Metal, is part of a thriving e-waste industry across Southeast Asia, born of China's decision
15 to stop accepting the world's electronic refuse, which was poisoning its land and people. Thailand in particular has become a center of the industry even as activists push back and its government wrestles to balance competing interests of public safety with the profits to be made from the lucrative
20 trade.

poisoning ～：～を汚染する

push back：反対する

competing interest of public safety with ～：～と競合する公共の安全利益

Last year, Thailand banned the import of foreign e-waste. Yet new factories are opening across the country, and tons of e-waste are being processed, environmental monitors and industry experts say.

environmental monitors：環境管理者

25 "E-waste has to go somewhere," said Jim Puckett, the executive director of the Basel Action Network, which campaigns against trash dumping in poor countries, "and the Chinese are simply moving their entire operations to Southeast Asia."

executive director：事務局長

trash dumping：ごみの投げ捨て

get huge volume with cheap, illegal labor：安い賃金で不法労働させて大量生産する

30 "The only way to make money is to get huge volume with cheap, illegal labor and pollute the hell out of the environment,"

the hell out of：徹底的に、ひどく

1-42

he added.

Each year, 50 million tons of electronic waste are produced globally, according to the United Nations, as consumers grow
35 accustomed to throwing away last year's model and acquiring the next new thing.

The notion of recycling these gadgets sounds virtuous: an infinite loop of technological utility.

But it is dirty and dangerous work to extract the tiny
40 quantities of precious metals — like gold, silver and copper — from castoff phones, computers and televisions.

For years, China took in much of the world's electronic refuse. Then in 2018, Beijing closed its borders to foreign e-waste. Thailand and other countries in Southeast Asia —
45 with their lax enforcement of environmental laws, easily exploited labor force and cozy nexus between business and government — saw an opportunity.

1-43

In June of last year, the Thai Ministry of Industry announced with great fanfare the ban on foreign e-waste.
50 The police made a series of high-profile raids on at least 10 factories, including New Sky Metal.

"New Sky is closed now, totally closed," Yutthana Poolpipat, the head of the Laem Chabang Port customs bureau, said in September. "There is no electronic waste coming into
55 Thailand, zero."

But a recent visit to the hamlet of Koh Khanun showed that the factory was still up and running, as are many others, a reflection of the weak regulatory system and corruption that has tainted the country.

The New York Times, December 8, 2019

virtuous：道徳にかなった

extract ～ from …：…から～を取り出す

castoff：廃棄処分された

lax enforcement：緩い適用

cozy nexus：結託した結びつき、癒着

made raids on ～：急襲した、手入れを行った

high-profile：人目を惹く

Laem Chabang Port：レムチャバン港《タイ中部にある同国を代表する港湾》

customs bureau：関税局

up and running：立ち上がって稼働している

reflection of ～：～を反映するもの

regulatory system：規制制度

corruption：汚職

tainted ～：～を汚染してきた

Exercises

次の１〜５の英文を完成させるために、ａ〜ｄの中から最も適切なものを１つ選びなさい。

1. The Chinese stopped recycling electronic scrap because

   a. it was a lucrative trade.

   b. it was employing too many people.

   c. it produced lower profits.

   d. it was poisoning their land.

2. Thailand's e-waste plants are dangerous because of

   a. smoke pouring over villages and farms.

   b. toxic fumes making people sick.

   c. the conditions in which people work.

   d. all of the above.

3. Corruption in the government of Thailand has

   a. allowed a few factories to continue operating.

   b. enabled the removal of all factories of e-waste.

   c. led to strictly enforced environmental laws.

   d. improved the air quality in places like Koh Khanun.

4. The Thai government

   a. denies any connection between e-waste and sickness.

   b. acknowledges the import of cheap illegal workers.

   c. openly welcomes any industry that makes large profits.

   d. officially bans the import of foreign e-waste.

5. Jim Puckett seems to be

   a. uninterested in the factories in Thailand.

   b. recommending the use of cheap illegal labor.

   c. an owner of an e-waste business.

   d. saying that it is difficult to control illegal e-waste industries.

本文の内容に合致するものに T（True）、合致しないものに F（False）をつけなさい。

(   )   **1.**   Thailand banned the import of e-waste last year.

(   )   **2.**   There has been a transfer of e-waste to poor countries in Southeast Asia.

(   )   **3.**   The main motive for e-waste processing is probably how lucrative the work is.

(   )   **4.**   The work is desirable and altruistic.

(   )   **5.**   The innards of computers, phones, or televisions have not been proven to be poison or poisonous.

Vocabulary

次 の 英文 は、the Japan Times に 掲載 さ れ た *"Throwaway society: Rejecting a life consumed by plastic'*『使い捨て社会：プラスティックが消費生活を拒絶する』 の 記事 の 一部です。下 の 語群 か ら 最 も 適切 な 語 を 1 つ 選 び、(   ) 内 に 記入 し な さ い。

Japan is (   ) for its use of disposable plastic. Elaborate but often (   ) food packaging is ubiquitous in supermarkets and convenience stores all over the country, and Japanese shoppers use an estimated 30 billion plastic shopping bags a year.

Japan is the world's (   )-biggest producer of plastic waste per capita behind the United States, and goes through around 9 million tons of plastic waste each year. Of that, more than 40 percent is (   ) plastic such as packaging and food containers.

"Whether you go to a convenience store or a supermarket, you basically have (   ) option but to use disposable plastic," says Hiroaki Odachi, project leader of Greenpeace Japan's plastic campaign. "Whatever you buy, it comes (   ) in packaging.

You don't need to spend long in Japan to notice how much single-use plastic there is, but is it really (   ) to avoid it? I decide to find out, and set myself a goal of not using any plastic that is designed to be (   ) away after a single use for a whole week.

disposable	impossible	infamous	no
second	thrown	unnecessary	wrapped

Unit **8**

● e スポーツがオリンピック後の日本を救うか？

「e スポーツ」のジャカルタ・アジア大会でインド選手と対戦する日本選手

Photo: Kyodo News

Before you read

1～7の「esports」のタイトルに該当するものを a ～ g の中から 1 つ選び、（　　　）内に記入しなさい。

1. Fighting games	（　　）	**a.**	multiplayer online battle arena
2. FPS	（　　）	**b.**	focusing on arcade play
3. MOBA	（　　）	**c.**	third person shooters
4. Racing	（　　）	**d.**	world cyber games
5. Real-time strategy	（　　）	**e.**	drivers race
6. Sports games	（　　）	**f.**	first person shooters
7. TPS	（　　）	**g.**	individuals competing on personal computers

次の1〜5の語の説明として最も近いものをa〜eから1つ選び、( )内に記入しなさい。

1. nascent　　　　( )　　a. use to gain a benefit
2. contagion　　　( )　　b. equally accessible to all
3. leverage　　　 ( )　　c. infection
4. aficionado　　 ( )　　d. new and still growing
5. egalitarian　　( )　　e. enthusiast

Summary

次の英文は記事の要約です。下の語群から最も適切な語を1つ選び、( ) 内に記入しなさい。

The postponement of the 2020 Olympics has been very ( ) for Japan, with COVID-19 ( ) sport in general because of restrictions on movement. Promoting esports could generate ( ) income. Neither physical contact nor physical ( ) is required, so this could ease the frustrations of sports-lovers of both genders and also ( ) the elderly in this aging society.

affecting　　attract　　costly　　much-needed　　strength

　　2020年3月に、新型コロナウイルスの感染拡大を受け、東京五輪・パラリンピックの延期が決まった。4か月後の開幕に向けて進んでいた準備が、大幅な見直しを迫られている。会場の再確保や人件費増大、資機材の保管料、追加経費など数千億円の規模になるのではないかと言われている。3月30日に東京五輪の開催日程が、2021年7月23日の金曜日に開会式を行い、8月8日日曜日に閉幕する17日間の日程となることが決まった。パラリンピックは8月24日から9月5日まで行われることになった。
　　東京五輪が1年後となり、Esports が日本人の模索している万能薬になるのではないか？さらに、新型コロナウイルスの感染拡大防止のため、密閉、密集、密接の3密禁止、外出自粛、social distancing を強いられているときに、esports こそ理想的な形ではないかと取り上げられるようになった。Esports とは「electronic sports エレクトロニック・スポーツ」のことで、電子機器を用いて行う娯楽・競技・スポーツ全般を言い、コンピューターゲーム、ビデオゲームを使ったスポーツ競技のことを指す。日本は世界から esports 後進国と呼ばれている。世界の競技人口は1億人以上、観戦者・視聴者3億8000万人だが、日本の競技人口は390万人、観戦者・視聴者は160万人しかないと言われている。

Reading

1-45

Can esports save post-Olympics Japan?

PROVIDENCE, RHODE ISLAND — The government recently announced an ambitious plan to nurture Japan's nascent esports industry. And both gamers and business leaders alike were left with a simple question: Why?

5　Surely right now — in this chaotic era of COVID-19 contagion and Olympic postponement — directing governmental resources at video games is at best tone deaf. And at worst, irresponsible.

1-46

After all, Japan is in crisis. With $13 billion sunk into the 10 Olympics, the decision to reschedule the games raises the costs by another $3 billion. Perhaps more importantly, postponing the Olympics has dealt a devastating blow to national morale that must be addressed. Compounding matters, the pandemic is already depressing travel and consumer spending. All these 15 factors solidify a 2020 recession as a certainty, with most analysts predicting Japanese GDP to decline by 1.1 percent or more.

And the current COVID-19 crisis does not exist in isolation. Rather, it is another woe heaped upon a country struggling 20 with deep systemic issues: including an aging population and endemic workplace sexism (as underscored by the #KuToo movement).

1-47

What could esports possibly have to do with all of these national challenges?

25　Everything. Esports may just be the total panacea Japan has been searching for.

First, let's discuss the Olympic hangover. Focusing on esports creates a smart opportunity to substitute one type of games for another. Around the world, professional leagues 30 like NASCAR, FIFA and the NBA are already leveraging esports content as replacement programming for traditional competitions.

esports：e スポーツ《複数のプレーヤーが参加するコンピュータゲームをスポーツとみなした表現》

PROVIDENCE：プロビデンス《米国ロードアイランド州の州都》

nurture 〜：〜を育成する

COVID-19：新型コロナウイルス感染症《coronavirus disease 2019》

contagion：伝染

postponement：延期

tone deaf：音痴《direct に（オーケストラを）指揮する意味もあるから》

morale：士気、気力

Compounding matters：事態を悪化させることに

pandemic：パンデミック、世界的大流行

recession：景気後退

GDP：国内総生産

sexism：性差別

#KuToo movement：KuToo 運動《日本の職場で女性がハイヒールおよびパンプスの着用を義務付けられていることに抗議する社会運動》ハリウッドの MeToo をもじって「靴」と「苦痛」を掛け合わせた》

have (everything) to do with 〜：〜と大いに関係がある《everything の代わりに What》

just：まさに

total panacea：万能薬

substitute 〜 for …：〜を…の代わりにする

NASCAR：全米自動車競走協会

FIFA：国際サッカー連盟

NBA：全米プロバスケットボール協会

46　Unit 8

Secondly, esports are the perfect social activity for a global pandemic. Video games do not require players to meet up in person or congregate in public. In fact, esports keep aficionados at home, while still generating meaningful economic activity in the form of game sales and micro-transactions. In fact, the gaming industry is growing as half the global population seeks entertainment while under lockdown orders.

But most of all, esports offer a much-needed morale boast to the beleaguered Japanese nation. Esports are something Japan should be good at. After all, the country essentially invented modern video games.

But the benefits of esports address more than just the current crisis. Competitive gaming also provides solutions to some of the fundamental, structural challenges facing the Japanese economy.

First and foremost among these is the aging population. Esports are a form of social interaction that can be enjoyed by gamers of all ages and ability levels. Envisioning a future of gaming grandmothers might seem ridiculous, but the problem of idle elderly is a real social issue. And esports don't just distract. Crucially, they keep both the mind and reflexes sharp — ameliorating the neurological decline threatening senior citizens.

Esports even address the nation's challenges with workplace sexism, albeit indirectly. As the world's first truly egalitarian sport, both men and women compete side by side at esports' highest levels.

Simply put, investing in esports makes strategic sense for Japan. Fostering this industry will provide meaningful solutions to both the immediate and societal challenges threatening the nation.

The Japan Times, April 11, 2020

---

aficionados：愛好家

micro-transactions： マイクロトランザクション《オンラインゲームなどで仮想世界の商品やサービスを少額で購入できるシステム》

First and foremost：何よりもまず

Envisioning 〜： 〜を心に描く

idle：何もすることがない

distract：気を紛らす

reflexes：反射神経

ameliorating 〜： 〜を改善させる

albeit 〜： 〜だが

egalitarian：（男女）平等主義の

Simply put：簡単に言うと

makes strategic sense：戦略的に有意義である

Fostering 〜： 〜を育てる

Exercises

次の1〜5の英文を完成させるために、a〜dの中から最も適切なものを1つ選びなさい。

1. The article starts off with

    a. reasons why esports would not be good for Japan.

    b. examples of how esports would be beneficial to Japan.

    c. how reasonable it seems to develop more esports.

    d. examples of the benefits of esports for developing countries.

2. The Olympics were postponed because of

    a. endemic workplace sexism.

    b. the danger Covid-19 posed to participants and spectators.

    c. the high morale of the country in anticipation of the Games.

    d. all of the above reasons.

3. Most financial individuals feel that recession in 2020 is

    a. highly unlikely.

    b. a certainty.

    c. a slim possibility.

    d. unlikely because of the Olympics.

4. The word "panacea" in the sixth paragraph probably means

    a. a drastic end to a problem.

    b. another word for a "recession."

    c. a solution or "cure all" to a problem.

    d. a correct understanding of a problem.

5. The author suggests esports could revitalize Japan because

    a. the large number of older citizens in the population lack gaming skills.

    b. men, women, the old and the young can all participate.

    c. they will encourage the elderly to take more physical exercise.

    d. esports are not competitive for most citizens.

True or False

本文の内容に合致するものに T (True)、合致しないものに F (False) をつけなさい。

(   ) **1.** The author is convinced that investing in esports will work towards easing economic and societal problems.

(   ) **2.** Esports would not help to keep aging minds alert or hone their reflexes.

(   ) **3.** Covid-19 has created a need to look for new ways to boost the economy.

(   ) **4.** It seems esports could benefit Japan's morale, as well as its economy.

(   ) **5.** The author begins with negative arguments about esports but ends up recommending them.

Vocabulary

次の 1 〜 8 は、「スポーツをする」という意味です。日本文に合わせて（   ）内に、適当な動詞を下の語群から 1 つ選び、必要があれば適当な形に直して記入しなさい。

1. 明日はゴルフをやろう。
Let's (   ) golfing tomorrow!

2. 霧の中で滑っていたら、スキーがとれてしまった。
While (   ) in fog, my ski came off.

3. やり投げの名人だ。
He is good at (   ) the javelin.

4. よくレスリングを週末毎にやった。
She used to (   ) every weekend.

5. ツール・ド・フランスで勝利した。
He (   ) to victory in the tour de France.

6. 3 時間以内でマラソンを完走した。
She (   ) the marathon within three hours

7. 体操の練習をやる予定だ。
He is going to (   ) some gymnastics exercises.

8. 高校の時勉強しないで、e スポーツをよくやった。
In high school I often (   ) esports without studying.

do	go	practice	ride
run	ski	throw	wrestle

疫病時にはアジア人でなくてもマスクした方がいいのか

新型コロナウイルス感染流行でベルギーのアントワープでも「マスク着用」を求める

Photo: Kyodo News

Before you read

a. ～ l. の顔の部位に該当するものをイラストの①～⑫の中から選びなさい。

a. cheek （　　　）
b. chin （　　　）
c. ear （　　　）
d. eye （　　　）
e. eyebrow （　　　）
f. eyelash （　　　）
g. forehead （　　　）
h. hair （　　　）
i. jaw （　　　）
j. lip （　　　）
k. mouth （　　　）
l. nose （　　　）

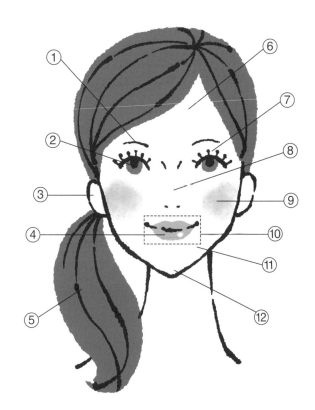

次の１～５の語の説明として最も近いものをａ～ｅから１つ選び、（　）内に記入しなさい。

1. exoticize   （　　）   **a.** make mysterious or strange

2. ward off   （　　）   **b.** block or prevent

3. defiant   （　　）   **c.** instruction or order

4. mitigate   （　　）   **d.** refusing to give in

5. directive   （　　）   **e.** make easier or weaker

Summary

次の英文は記事の要約です。下の語群から最も適切な語を１つ選び、（　）内に記入しなさい。

While face masks have (　　　　　) been worn in Japan, use has increased there and spread to neighboring parts of Asia. This has led some people to (　　　　　) masks as part of Asian culture. As the direct medical (　　　　　) of masks are still unclear, there may be some truth in this (　　　　　). But the messages of self-restraint and solidarity that masks send may also be (　　　　　) in crises.

beneficial   benefits   long   perceive   perception

　　日本では、冬から春にかけて、マスクはインフルエンザ、大気汚染、花粉症に悩む人たちにとっての必需品だった。明治時代には炭鉱で働く人たちが粉塵除けに真鍮製の金網を芯に、布地をフィルターとして取り付けたものだった。その後1918年に「スペイン・カゼ」が猛威をふるい、予防品としてマスクが着用された。当時、国のポスターに「マスクをかけぬ命知らず！」と書かれ、黒いマスクをつけた紳士と婦人が描かれている。以後インフルエンザや風邪が流行するたびにマスクが着用されている。1970年代の公害、80年代の花粉症の流行もマスクの普及となった。マスクの着用は、周囲への思いやりとエチケットでもあり、またリスクや不安から逃れるための安心感でもある。

　　しかし、欧米諸国では感染者や疑似感染者だけが着用を義務付けられ、重病人用の医療用品だと思われている。2020年２月末に英国の新型コロナウイルス感染者は100人台だったが、ロンドンの地下鉄では、マスク着用の私の周りには誰も寄って来なかった。フランスでは、３月に不着用者には約16,000円の罰金が課せられた。アメリカでは、犯罪者がマスクやバンダナなどで身元を隠すと言われ、18州では、理由なしに公共の場でマスクをつけること自体が違法という「反マスク法」と呼ばれる法律がある。黒人と白人のマスク着用では意味が違うようだが、感染防止のためのマスクが偏見や差別をもたらしてもいる。

Reading

1-51

You don't have to be Asian to wear a face mask in an epidemic

epidemic：疫病、伝染病

FUKUOKA — It's important to understand the many reasons why East Asians have increasingly been wearing face masks over the past two decades — but there are some good reasons not to exoticize, or stigmatize face mask wearing as a
5 culturally "Asian" practice.

stigmatize 〜 as …：〜は …だと烙印を押す

1-52

In this instance, assumptions about cultural difference are easy enough to confirm. Face mask-wearing has become ubiquitous in East Asian societies. When I first began teaching in Japan in the spring of 2000, I noticed that some students
10 were wearing them, which they explained were for pollen allergies. Use of face masks has grown dramatically in the past decade, however. According to Nippon.com, production of face masks for personal use rose from 500 million in 2011 to 4.4 billion in 2018.

assumptions：思い込み、決 めてかかること

ubiquitous：あちこちで目に する

which they explained were：which は wearing masks ではなく masks を指 す

pollen：花粉

Nippon.com：ニッポンドッ トコム《日本情報多言語 発信サイト》

1-53
15 There are a number of explanations for this rapid rise in usage. Those explanations refer to government influenza advisories and mass media influencing trends to wear masks as a protection for the healthy and as an etiquette for the unwell, to the subtle social pressures to conform which accelerate
20 such trends, and to clever marketing strategies which further normalize those trends, including the promotion of masks as fashion accessories to young women.

refer to 〜：〜に言及する 《to 〜が３つある》

the healthy：健康な人たち 《the ＋形容詞》

conform：同調する

normalize 〜：〜を常態に する

1-54
Throughout East Asia masks are also increasingly used to ward off colds and viruses or to protect others from them, as
25 protection from air pollution, and as fashion accessories, much like they are in Japan. As medical anthropologist Christos Lynteris pointed out in The New York Times, their use is also a social ritual, a means for expressing and performing solidarity and a common sense of belonging in a crisis. And
30 not only in epidemic crises, as was strikingly illustrated by the defiant crowds of masked protesters in Hong Kong's pro-

ward off 〜：〜を防ぐ

medical anthropologist： 医療人類学者

solidarity：団結、結束

common sense of belonging：共通の相互 信頼感

as：《関係代名詞：先行詞は solidarity 以下》

pro-democracy：民主化を 求める

democracy movement.

But, the inevitable question arises: outside of standard clinical or emergency medicine settings, do face masks 35 assist in slowing virus transmission? Here, the jury is still out. Following the SARS epidemic, researchers pointed to a lack of multivariate, case-control research demonstrating the efficacy of widespread mask usage by healthy people in epidemic conditions — and there are ethical problems 40 inherent in conducting such research.

However, defenders of more widespread public use of face masks during epidemics invoke some evidence that such a measure provides moderate self- and community protection against virus transmission. They also highlight evidence 45 of pre- and asymptomatic transmission of coronavirus as support for recommendations that even healthy people wear face masks when going out in public.

Let's forget the culturalist nonsense that there are distinctively "Asian" approaches to mitigating and containing 50 epidemics, including public face mask usage. Should everyone be wearing them? Thinking of the health and even lives of millions that are now at stake, I consider it smart as a layperson to follow expert and government advice concerning measures like social distancing, personal hygiene maintenance 55 and face mask wearing, and to obey more drastic containment directives, should they come into effect.

The Japan Times, March 17, 2020

transmission：伝染

Here：今の時点では

the jury is still out：まだ結論は出ていない

SARS：重症急性呼吸器症候群

case-control research：症例対照研究

efficacy：有効性

inherent in 〜：〜に付いて回る

defenders：擁護者

pre- and asymptomatic：発症前の、そして無症状期の

mitigating 〜：〜を和らげる

containing：〜を封じ込める

at stake：危機にさらされている

layperson：素人、門外漢

hygiene maintenance：清潔維持

directives：指示、命令

should they come into effect：効力があれば

1-55

Exercises

次の１〜５の英文を完成させるために、ａ〜ｄの中から最も適切なものを１つ選びなさい。

1. Face masks were worn originally

   a. for individuals who have allergies or a cold.
   b. as a fashion accessory.
   c. to do what everybody else does.
   d. by protestors in Hong Kong.

2. Now face masks are being worn

   a. for protection from others carrying the Covid-19 virus.
   b. to protect others if you have a cold or the flu.
   c. as a fashion accessory.
   d. for all of the above reasons.

3. Other ways doctors recommend avoiding becoming ill include

   a. good personal hygiene, including frequent washing of hands.
   b. going outside when instructed by authorities.
   c. concealing your identity during political demonstrations.
   d. all of the above World Health Organization instructions.

4. The production of face masks has gone from

   a. 4.4 million to 5 billion.
   b. 5 million to 20.1 billion.
   c. 50 million to 4.4 billion.
   d. 500 million to 4.4 billion.

5. The government in Japan is wisely advising its citizens to

   a. protect themselves only when unwell.
   b. protect themselves even if they feel healthy.
   c. wear fashionable masks.
   d. follow all of the above.

本文の内容に合致するものに T（True）、合致しないものに F（False）をつけなさい。

(　　) **1.** The use of face masks has not risen in Asia.

(　　) **2.** The people who are wearing masks for allergies might not be contagious to others.

(　　) **3.** If more serious measures for protection are given, they must be followed by all to be effective.

(　　) **4.** No one is sure if masks protect against virus spread.

(　　) **5.** Healthy citizens should not wear a mask during a pandemic.

Vocabulary

次の英文は、The New York Times に掲載された *Mask-Wearing, Common in Asia, Spreads in the West*『マスク着用、アジアでは普通だったが、欧米では広まっている』の記事の一部です。下の語群から最も適切なものを１つ選び、(　　　) 内に記入しなさい。

Until a few weeks ago, Asian tourists were the (　　　　) mask-wearers in Paris, eliciting puzzlement or (　　　　) from French locals, or even hostility as the coronavirus began sweeping across Europe.

Four days into a national lockdown to stem the outbreak, the French government spokeswoman, Sibeth Ndiaye, warned that face masks were so (　　　　) that wearing them was too difficult technically and could even be "counterproductive." Even on Thursday morning, when asked whether she wore a mask or made her children (　　　　) one, she said, "Oh, no, not at all."

This taboo is falling fast, not only in France but across Western countries, after mounting cries from experts who say the practice is (　　　　) in curbing the coronavirus pandemic.

The shift for Western nations is profound and has had to overcome not merely the logistical challenges of (　　　　) enough masks, which are significant enough, but also a deep (　　　　) resistance and even stigma associated with mask-wearing, which some Western leaders described flatly as "alien."

cultural	effective	only	securing
suspicion	unfamiliar	wear	

Unit 10

●他の人たちよりもずっと感染力が強い人たちがいる理由

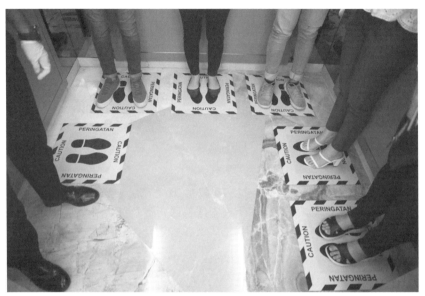

新型コロナウイルス感染流行でインドネシアではエレベーター内の立ち位置を指定

Photo: AP ／アフロ

Before you read

　1～7の「epidemic 疫病」に関連するものをa～gの中から1つ選び、（　　　）内に記入しなさい。

1. plague　ペスト　　　　　　　　　（　　）　　　**a.** Spanish influenza
2. Spanish Flu　スペイン風邪　　　（　　）　　　**b.** vaccination
3. tuberculosis　結核　　　　　　　（　　）　　　**c.** Covid-19
4. smallpox　天然痘　　　　　　　 （　　）　　　**d.** found in soil
5. tetanus　破傷風　　　　　　　　（　　）　　　**e.** Black Death
6. coronavirus　コロナウイルス　 （　　）　　　**f.** Robert Koch
7. cholera　コレラ　　　　　　　　（　　）　　　**g.** contaminated water

次の１〜５の語句の説明として最も近いものをa〜eから１つ選び、（　　）内に記入しなさい。

1. infectious （　　） a. vulnerable
2. at play （　　） b. sudden and expansive emergence
3. misattribute （　　） c. contributory or relevant
4. outbreak （　　） d. connect falsely
5. susceptible （　　） e. likely to pass on to someone else

Summary

次の英文は記事の要約です。下の語群から最も適切な語を１つ選び、（　　）内に記入しなさい。

Some people seem to spread illnesses more (　　　　　) than others. In Hong Kong, a (　　　　　) small number transmitted SARS to a relatively large number. The (　　　　　) was true of Ebola in Africa. (　　　　　), most MERS-sufferers in Korea did not pass on the disease. Understanding the reasons for the differences is complex, involving (　　　　　) study of matters such as social behavior.

1-56

close　　conversely　　easily　　relatively　　same

　2019年11月17日に中華人民共和国湖北省出身の男性が新型コロナウイルスの最初の症例だったと South China Morning Post が報じている。しかし、実際には11月22日に湖北省武漢市で「原因不明のウイルス性肺炎」として最初の症例が確認された。武漢市内の武漢華南海鮮卸売市場で同定され、それ以降、武漢市内から中国大陸へ感染が広がり、187以上の国々に感染が広がった。20年８月10日現在感染者数2,040万人を上回り、死亡者数74.4万、回復者数1,263万である。世界各国の主要都市で都市封鎖や移動制限の Lockdown が実施され、社会的・経済的に大きな損益を及ぼしている。

　日本では新型コロナウイルスと呼んでいるが、正式には SARS-CoV-2（Severe acute respiratory syndrome coronavirus version 2）と命名された。しかし欧米のメディアでは、Covid-19を使っている。中国浙江省舟山市のコウモリから発見された SARS ウイルスとの類似度を持つと言われている。コロナウイルスには複数の型があり、武漢市の大流行はL型で全体の７割を占める。S型は全体の３割でコウモリ由来のウイルスに近い。

　日本でも20年４月17日に全国に「緊急事態宣言」が出され、手洗いの徹底、マスク着用、social distancing, 密接・密閉・密集の３密の回避を徹する「新しい生活様式」が促されている。その後、５月25日をもって日本全国で「緊急事態宣言」が解除された。しかし、８月12日の全国の感染者数が５万人を超えた。

1-57

Why Are Some People So Much More Infectious Than Others?

> Solving the mystery of "superspreaders" could help control the coronavirus pandemic.

Distinguishing between those who are more infectious and those less infectious could make an enormous difference in the ease and speed with which an outbreak is contained, said Jon Zelner, an epidemiologist at the University of Michigan.
5 If the infected person is a superspreader, contact tracing is especially important. But if the infected person is the opposite of a superspreader, someone who for whatever reason does not transmit the virus, contact tracing can be a wasted effort.

1-58
"The tricky part is that we don't necessarily know who
10 those people are," Dr. Zelner said.

Two factors are at play, said Martina Morris, emeritus professor of statistics and sociology at the University of Washington.

"There has to be a link between people in order to transmit
15 an infection," she said. But, she added, a link "is necessary but not sufficient." The second factor is how infectious a person is. "We almost never have independent data on those two things," Dr. Morris said.

She pointed out that it can be easy to misattribute multiple
20 infections to an individual — possibly exposing the person to public attack — when the spread has nothing to do with the person's infectiousness.

1-59
Yet there do seem to be situations in which a few individuals spark large outbreaks.

25 In 2003 during the SARS outbreak, the first patient in Hong Kong appears to have infected at least 125 others. Other superspreading events involved 180 people in a housing complex in Hong Kong and another 22 people on a jet from Hong Kong to Beijing.

superspreaders：スーパー・スプレッダー、超感染拡大者

Distinguishing between 〜 and …：〜と…との違いが分かる

make a difference in 〜：〜において効果がある

ease：容易さ

contained：阻止される

epidemiologist：疫学者、伝染病学者

contact tracing：接触者追跡

tricky：扱いにくい

at play：登場する

emeritus professor：名誉教授

statistics：統計学

independent：独自の

misattribute 〜 to …：誤って〜を…のせいにする

multiple infections：多重感染

public attack：公然たる非難

do seem：《動詞の強調》

SARS：サーズ（重症急性呼吸器症候群）

housing complex：団地

30 　　In the Ebola outbreak in Africa between 2014 and 2016, 61 percent of infections were traced to just 3 percent of infected people.

1-60

　　At the other end of the bell curve of infectiousness are infected people who do not seem to infect others. During the
35 MERS outbreak in South Korea, 89 percent of patients did not appear to transmit the disease.

　　In the Covid-19 pandemic, there is a striking example from the far end of uninfectious — a couple in Illinois.

　　On Jan. 23 the wife, who had returned from a visit
40 to Wuhan, became the first laboratory-confirmed case of Covid-19 in the state. On Jan. 30, her husband was infected. It was the first known person-to-person transmission in the United States.

1-61

　　Both husband and wife became gravely ill and were
45 hospitalized. Both recovered. State public health officials traced their contacts — 372 people, including 195 health care workers. Not a single one became infected.

　　Dr. Jennifer Layden, chief medical officer for the Chicago Department of Public Health, said the remarkable lack of
50 spread probably arose from several factors. Where were the couple in the course of their infection when they came into contact with those other people? Were they sneezing or coughing? How close were the contacts? Were the people they interacted with simply less susceptible to infections?

The New York Times, April 12, 2020

Ebola：エボラ出血熱

bell curve：ベル（釣鐘）型曲線

are infected people：《副詞句の強調による倒置：infected people are》

MERS：マーズ（中東呼吸器症候群）

Covid-19：新型コロナウイルス感染症

uninfectious：非感染症の、感染を引き起こすことのできない

Wuhan：武漢

laboratory-confirmed：検査で確認された

public health officials：公衆衛生当局

chief medical officer：医務部長

Where：どの段階に

in the course of ～：～の過程の

sneezing：くしゃみする

close：濃厚な、近づいて

interacted with ～：～と関わった

susceptible to ～：～にかかり易い、～に影響を受ける

Exercises

次の１～３の英文の質問に答え、４～５の英文を完成させるために、ａ～ｄの中から最も適切なものを１つ選びなさい。

1. What makes contact tracing both important and a waste of time?

    a. Incomplete calculations of data.
    b. Finding a superspreader.
    c. Finding an infected person who does not spread the virus.
    d. None of the above.

2. What percentage of Ebola infections came from what percentage of infected people?

    a. 3% from 61% of infected people.
    b. 19% from 3% of infected people.
    c. 61% from 29% of infected people.
    d. 61% from 3% of infected people.

3. A woman returning from Wuhan infected her husband. How many others were infected by them?

    a. Only two.
    b. 372 people.
    c. None.
    d. There is no data on their contacts.

4. During the SARS outbreak, the first person in Hong Kong infected

    a. 22 people.
    b. 80 people.
    c. 125 people.
    d. 180 people.

5. Possible reasons for non-infection of others from the first woman returning from Wuhan are

    a. lack of close the contacts with the people.
    b. absence of coughs and sneezes when meeting their contact.
    c. the low susceptible of the contacts themselves.
    d. all of the above.

本文の内容に合致するものに T (True)、合致しないものに F (False) をつけなさい。

(   ) **1.** In South Korea in the MERS epidemic, 89% of the people tested were found not to transmit the disease.

(   ) **2.** The "superspreader" mystery being solved might help control the Covid-19 problem.

(   ) **3.** People can become infected even while flying on a plane.

(   ) **4.** Finding out who is more infectious is not relevant to the outbreak.

(   ) **5.** This article mentions patients who unfortunately died.

Vocabulary

次の英文は、the New York Times に掲載された *How to Save Black and Hispanic Lives in a Pandemic*『世界的に広がっている伝染病から黒人とヒスパニック系の人々を救う方法』の記事の一部です。下の語群から最も適切な語を 1 つ選び、(   ) 内に記入しなさい。

Across the United States, black and Hispanic people suffer disproportionately from (   ), poor health care and (   ) diseases like diabetes, hypertension and asthma.

As the pandemic continues, it is crucial that local and state health departments across the country report data on how the coronavirus is (   ) people by (   ) and also by gender and age.

The racial disparities may be predictable, but they are (   ) nonetheless. Public health experts say there are actions that states and cities can take right now to help (   ) lives. Doing so would help protect all vulnerable people.

The country's response to the pandemic remains (   ) by medical supply shortages. As masks, gloves and other protective equipment become more available, it is clear that all essential workers require them, not just emergency and medical personnel. That includes janitors, home health aides, delivery people, grocery and farm workers and sanitation workers. In New York City, as in many cities, much of the municipal (   ) force is black or Hispanic.

affecting	chronic	hampered	poverty
race	save	tragic	work

Unit 11

● 疫病の渦中で必要なのはフランスではペイストリーとワイン、米国ではゴルフと銃

新型コロナウイルス感染流行でもフランスは飲食店再開。前を通り過ぎる人たちはマスクを着用
Photo: ロイター／アフロ

Before you read

1. What do you think the article will be about?

   この記事は何の話題についてだと思いますか？

2. What is essential for you in the middle of an epidemic?

   疫病の渦中であなたにとって必要なものは何ですか？

次の 1〜5 の語句の説明として最も近いものを a〜e から 1 つ選び、(　　) 内に記入しなさい。

1. bid　　　　　　　　(　　)　　a. collapse into chaos
2. exempt　　　　　　(　　)　　b. illness
3. a good deal of　　(　　)　　c. attempt
4. ailment　　　　　 (　　)　　d. excepted
5. breakdown　　　　(　　)　　e. much

Summary

次の英文は記事の要約です。下の語群から最も適切な語を 1 つ選び、(　　) 内に記入しなさい。

1-62

In response to the novel coronavirus governments throughout the world (　　　　　　) business activity, while granting (　　　　　) to services considered essential.　But ideas about what is essential (　　　　　) considerably.　Guns and golf seem to be (　　　　) for many Americans. Praying outside is important to Israelis.　And (　　　　　), the French prioritize wine and fine food.

| exceptions | necessary | restricted | unsurprisingly | vary |

　2020年 3 月25日、新型コロナウイルスの感染拡大防止のため、都知事が週末や夜間の不要不急の外出、飲食を伴う会合の自粛などを要請した。4 月 8 日に 7 都府県を対象に『緊急事態宣言』が出され、17日には日本全国に拡大した。不要不急の外出などを控える自粛生活へと突入した。2 月頃から、国民も「巣ごもり」姿勢を強めていた。

　5 月 8 日に総務省が 3 月の家計調査を発表した。飲食関係では、長期保存可能な食品への買いだめ需要が高まり、パスタ（44.4％増）や即席めん（30.6％増）、チュウハイ・カクテル（22.8％増）が伸びた。しかし、自宅外での外食代（30.3％減）、飲酒代（53.5％減）が減少した。自宅での娯楽用としてのゲーム機は、165.8％も増え、2019年 3 月の消費額に比べて2.7倍になった。テレワークによる在宅勤務や動画配信サービスの需要増などで「インターネット接続料」も12.4％増加した。

　自宅用としてトイレットペーパー買いだめのため26.4％増、体温計75.6％と跳ね上がった。3 密回避、「外出自粛」のため、映画、旅行、ガソリン、航空運賃、鉄道通勤・通学定期代などの消費が大幅に減少した。

Reading

What's essential? In France, pastry and wine – in the US, golf and guns

| Some activities reflect a national identity. |

The coronavirus pandemic is defining for the world what is "essential" and what things we really cannot do without, even though we might not need them for survival.

Authorities in many places are determining what shops and services can remain open, in a bid to slow the spread of the virus.

Whether it is in Asia, Europe, Africa or the United States, there is general agreement – health care workers, law enforcement, utility workers, food production and communications are generally exempt from lockdowns.

But some lists of exempted activities reflect a national identity, or the efforts of lobbyists.

In some US states, golf, guns and marijuana have been ruled essential, raising eyebrows and, in the case of guns, a good deal of ire.

"Recent events clearly demonstrate that the process of designating 'essential services' is as much about culture as any legal-political reality about what is necessary to keep society functioning," said Christopher McKnight Nichols, associate professor of history at Oregon State University, in the US.

Countries including India and US states are listing the information technology sector as essential.

The world's dependency on the internet has become even more apparent as countless people confined to their homes communicate, stream movies and play games online to stave off cabin fever.

Several states where marijuana is legal, such as California and Washington, deemed pot shops and workers in the market's supply chain essential.

"Cannabis is a safe and effective treatment that millions

---

national identity：国民性

defining ～：～の意味を明らかにする

for the world：絶対に、断じて

do without ～：～無しですます

Authorities：行政官庁

in a bid to ～：～の措置として

law enforcement：（警察などの）法執行機関

utility workers：作業員

exempt from ～：～が適用されない、免除される

lobbyists：ロビイスト《ロビー活動とは、特定の主張を有する個人または団体が政府の政策に影響を及ぼすことを目的として行う詩的な政治活動》

ruled：規定される

raising eyebrows：人を驚かせる

ire：憤激（させる）

designating ～：～を指定する

stave off ～：～を回避する

cabin fever：ストレス

deemed ～ …：～を…と判断した

pot：マリファナ

Cannabis：大麻

of Americans rely on to maintain productive daily lives while suffering from diseases and ailments," Erik Altieri, executive director of the National Organisation for the Reform of Marijuana Laws, said.

35 Texas attorney general Ken Paxton issued a legal opinion saying emergency orders in his state cannot restrict gun sales.

1-66

"If you have a breakdown in society, well then our first line to defend ourselves is ourselves, so I think having a weapon is very important for your personal safety," Texas lieutenant

40 governor Dan Patrick told a radio interviewer.

In Arizona, governor Doug Ducey included golf courses on his list. Officials in Phoenix encouraged the city's 1.7 million residents to "get outside, get exercise and practice responsible social distancing" in golf courses, parks and trails.

45 In Europe, the current epicentre of the pandemic, Italy has the most stringent rules, with only essential businesses such as food shops and pharmacies remaining open.

1-67

The manufacturing sector was ordered shut down on Thursday, though factories that make needed products

50 like medical supplies will continue to operate after making conditions safer for employees.

In France, shops specialising in pastry, wine and cheese have been declared essential businesses.

In a nod to Israel's vibrant religious life, people can gather

55 for outdoor prayers, with a maximum of 10 worshippers standing two metres apart.

Aimee Huff, marketing professor at Oregon State University, specialising in consumer culture, said: "In times of uncertainty, institutions and practices that are central to the

60 cultural identities can become really important touchstones, material markers of certainty, comfort, and mechanisms to persist."

The Express & Star, March 19, 2020

---

ailments：（軽い）慢性病

National Organisation for the Reform of Marijuana Laws：マリファナ法改正を求める全国組織

attorney general：（州の）司法長官

restrict ～：～を制限する

breakdown：機能停止

lieutenant governor：州副知事

encouraged ～ to …：～に…すよう奨励した

trails：未舗装道路、小道、田舎道

epicentre：震源地

pharmacies：薬局

medical supplies：医療用品

In a nod to ～：～を考慮して

prayers：祈り

touchstones：試金石、基準《become の補語は touchstones, markers そして mechanisms の3つ》

markers：標識

mechanisms：仕組み

persist：存続する

Exercises

次の、1～2の英文の質問に答え、3～5の英文を完成させるために、a～dの中から最も適切なものを1つ選びなさい。

1. While being in lockdown position, which essentials are somewhat surprising?

    a. Golfs, guns, and marijuana in parts of the US.

    b. The importance of the Internet and IT in India and the US.

    c. Food in various parts of Europe.

    d. Health care work around the world.

2. In what country would you see groups of 10 in prayer standing 2 metres apart?

    a. India.

    b. Pakistan.

    c. Israel.

    d. Myanmar.

3. For a long period during the Covid-19 pandemic in Italy

    a. shops were closed but large restaurants stayed open.

    b. all shops except grocery stores and pharmacies were closed.

    c. shops remained open but citizens had to stay home for many weeks.

    d. only the opera halls were closed.

4. The essential cultural necessities in France are

    a. cheese and rice.

    b. wine and bread.

    c. pastry and pasta.

    d. cheese, pastry and wine.

5. This article explains that

    a. in crises people desire things that are unfamiliar and exciting.

    b. different items allow people to feel comfortable in different cultures.

    c. scientists have found that people can exist without cultural foods and items.

    d. most people prioritize luxurious things in a crisis.

本文の内容に合致するものに T（True）、合致しないものに F（False）をつけなさい。

(　) **1.** Some activities or items or food are considered necessary by citizens but they do not ensure their survival of Covid-19 virus.

(　) **2.** Some items show national identity, like French emphasis on wine, cheese, and pastries.

(　) **3.** Not everyone in the U.S. feels guns, golf, and marijuana are comforting items.

(　) **4.** The Texas Attorney General is not in favor of guns and wants extra restrictions on gun sales.

(　) **5.** Italy was forced into closing factories that make the medical supplies needed during a pandemic.

Vocabulary

次の 1 ～ 7 は、「Coronavirus」に関する英文です。日本文に合わせて、適当な語を下の語群から 1 つ選び、（　　　）内に記入しなさい。

1. 飲食を伴う宴会は控えて頂きますようお願いします。
We request that you (　　　　　) from parties accompanied by eating and drinking.

2. 政府により、緊急事態宣言が出された。
A state of (　　　　　) declaration is called by the government.

3. 特に不要不急の仕事の場合は、できるだけ在宅勤務をお願いします。
The authorities ask that people work from home as much as possible, especially if your work is considered (　　　　　) and nonurgent.

4. 政府は、海外への渡航の自粛をお願いしています。
The government has now asked people here to refrain from travel (　　　　　).

5. 新型コロナウイルスの感染拡大のため、2020年の東京オリンピックは延期になった。
Due to the spread of infection from the novel coronavirus, the 2020 Tokyo Olympics is (　　　　　).

6. 自粛ムードは、経済にも影響している。
The air of (　　　　　) has also had an effect on the economy.

7. 感染拡大で日経平均株価が下落する。
The Nikkei Stock Average goes down as the (　　　　　) of contagion rises.

emergency	nonessential	overseas	postponed
refrain	self-restraint	spread	

Unit 12

● iPhone のはるか前に無線社会の基礎を築いた人たち

電池で科学技術の将来を築いたノーベル化学賞受賞者たち（写真は左から吉野さん、グッドイナフ氏そしてウィッテンガム氏）　　Photo: TT News Agency／アフロ

Before you read

Kingdom of Sweden
スウェーデン王国

面積　450,000km^2（日本の約1.2倍）（世界57位）
人口　10,220,000人（世界91位）
公用語　スウェーデン語
首都　ストックホルム
民族　スウェーデン人　85%
　　　フィンランド人　5％
宗教　キリスト教プロテスタント・ルター派80%
GDP　5,560億ドル（世界23位）
　　　１人当たりGDP　54,356ドル（世界12位）
通貨　スウェーデン・クローネ
政体　立憲君主制
識字率　99%

次の１～５の語の説明として最も近いものをa～eから１つ選び、（　）内に記入しなさい。

1. rechargeable　（　　）　　　**a.** network

2. grid　　　　　（　　）　　　**b.** electrical conductor

3. sustainable　 （　　）　　　**c.** able to be filled or activated again

4. bulky　　　　 （　　）　　　**d.** using renewable resources

5. electrode　　 （　　）　　　**e.** large and awkward

次の英文は記事の要約です。下の語群から最も適切な語を１つ選び、（　）内に記入しなさい。

1-68

　Compact lithium batteries are (　　　　　　) in many of the electronic devices we use daily.　Now the men who (　　　　　) the technology, enabling Sony to develop batteries (　　　　　), have been honored with a Nobel prize.　Scientists Goodenough, Whittingham and Yoshino played key roles in (　　　　　) the use of this super-light metal as an electrical (　　　　).

commercially　　conductor　　indispensable　　pioneered　　promoting

　2019年のノーベル化学賞は、吉野彰・旭化成名誉フェローと、テキサス大のジョン・グッドイナフ教授、ニューヨーク州立大のスタンリー・ウィッティンガム卓越教授に授与された。「リチウムイオン電池の開発」が授賞理由だ。リチウムイオン電池は、小型で軽量、高出力で、何度も充電でき、何度も使えるのが特徴である。スマートフォンやノートパソコンなどのモバイル機器や電気自動車などに広く使われ、現代社会の礎を築いたとされる。

　1970年代に、ウィッティンガム氏がプラス極に二硫化チタン、マイナス極に金属リチウムを使った電池を開発した。しかし、金属リチウムは他の物質と反応して発熱する危険があり、実用には至らなかった。80年代にグッドイナフ氏と東大助手として留学していた水島公一・東芝エグゼクティブフェローが、プラス極にコバルト酸リチウムを用いた電池を作製した。この電池の寿命はわずか数日だったが、約４ボルトの電圧を発生できた。

　1985年、吉野氏は電気を通すプラスチック「ポリアセチレン」をマイナス極に使い、プラス極にはグッドイナフ氏らのコバルト酸リチウムを用いた。さらに旭化成が開発した特殊な炭素繊維をマイナス極に使って、小型化する方法も開発し、現在のリチウムイオン電池の原型を完成させた。大容量で小型電池をさらに進めた次世代電池は、IT機器、電気自動車、AI、ロボット、通信技術の発達の鍵を握るだろう。

Reading

1-69

They Laid Foundation For a Wireless Society

▍ Long Before iPhones ▍

The Royal Swedish Academy of Sciences awarded the 2019 Nobel Prize in Chemistry on Wednesday to three scientists who developed lithium-ion batteries, which have revolutionized portable electronics.

5　　John B. Goodenough, M. Stanley Whittingham and Akira Yoshino will share the prize, which is worth about $900,000.

1-70

　　The three researchers' work in the 1970s and '80s led to the creation of powerful, lightweight and rechargeable batteries used in nearly every smartphone or laptop computer,
10 and in billions of cameras and power tools. Astronauts on the International Space Station rely on them, and engineers working on renewable energy grids often turn to them.

　　M. Stanley Whittingham, 77, a professor at Binghamton University, State University of New York, and one of the three
15 winners, said that he always hoped lithium-ion technology would grow, "but we never envisaged it growing this far. We never imagined it being ubiquitous in things like iPhones."

1-71

　　John B. Goodenough, 97, is a professor at the University of Texas at Austin. With the award he becomes the oldest
20 Nobel Prize winner, but is still active in research.

　　And Akira Yoshino, 71, is an honorary fellow for the Asahi Kasei Corporation in Tokyo and a professor at Meijo University in Nagoya, Japan. He said after the announcement that he was pleased that the technology could also help fight
25 climate change, calling lithium-ion batteries "suitable for a sustainable society."

　　The first rechargeable battery came about in 1859. These were made from lead-acid, and are still used to start gasoline- and diesel-powered vehicles today. But lead-acid batteries
30 were bulky and heavy. Nickel-cadmium batteries, which were less efficient but more compact, were invented in 1899.

Royal Swedish Academy of Science：スウェーデン王立科学アカデミー

lithium-ion batteries：リチウムイオン電池《イオンとは、電子の過剰あるいは欠損により電荷を帯びた原子または原子団》

electronics：電子機器

Akira Yoshino：吉野彰

rechargeable：再充電可能な

power tools：電動工具

renewable energy grids：再生可能なエネルギー供給網

Binghamton University：ビンガムトン大学《ニューヨーク州立大学を構成する大学の一つ》

envisaged ～：～を心に思い描く、想像する

Asahi Kasei Corporation：旭化成株式会社

Meijo University：名城大学

climate change：気候変動

sustainable society：持続可能な社会《国連の提唱する概念：将来の世代の欲求を損ねることなく、現在の世代の欲求も満足させる社会》

lead-acid：鉛酸

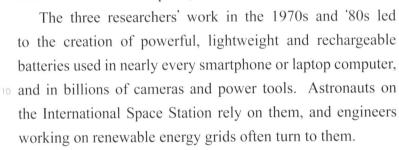

For many years, there were no major advancements in battery technology. But the Arab oil embargo of 1973 made many scientists realize the extent of society's dependence on
35 fossil fuels. Dr. Whittingham, who was working for Exxon at the time, began searching for improved ways to store energy from renewable sources and power electric cars.

He knew that lithium would make a good anode because it released electrons easily. It also had the advantage of being
40 the lightest metal. So Dr. Whittingham started looking for materials that had a high energy density and captured lithium-ions in the cathode — the side of your battery with the plus sign.

Dr. Whittingham discovered that titanium disulfide, which
45 had never been used in batteries before, had a molecular structure that let lithium-ions into small pockets. This resulted in the first functional lithium battery.

Dr. Goodenough, then at Oxford, predicted that lithium-ion batteries would have greater potential if the cathode were
50 made with a different material. He noticed that cobalt oxide was similar in structure to titanium disulfide.

Building from Dr. Goodenough's work, Dr. Yoshino, who was at the Asahi Kasei Corporation in Japan, then showed that more complicated carbon-based electrodes could house
55 lithium-ions in between their layers too.

These developments ultimately led to commercialization of the lithium-ion battery in 1991 by another Japanese electronics giant, Sony Corporation.

The New York Times International Edition, October 10, 2019

embargo：禁輸措置	
fossil fuels：化石燃料	
Exxon：エクソン《現在の エクソン・モービル：世界 最大の民間石油会社》	
power ～：～に動力・電力 を供給する	
anode：（電池の場合の）負 極	
high energy density：高エ ネルギー密度	
cathode：（電池の場合の） 正極	
plus sign：＋（プラス）記号	
titanium disulfide：二硫化 チタン	
molecular structure：分子 構造	
pockets：くぼみ、穴	
potential：電位	
cobalt oxide：酸化コバル ト	
Building from ～：～を発 展させて	
carbon-based electrodes： 炭素系電極	
house ～ in …：～を…に 収納する	
between their layers：層間	
electronics giant：電子工 業大手	

Exercises

Multiple Choice

次の１〜５の英文を完成させるために、 ａ〜ｄの中から最も適切なものを１つ選びなさい。

1. The three scientists who received the Nobel Prize in Chemistry

    a. all came from the same country and worked together.

    b. came from New York, Texas, and Japan but contributed to the same goal.

    c. are receiving the prize at an early stage in their careers.

    d. all went to the same university together.

2. The battery that could have a positive impact for a sustainable society is

    a. the lithium-ion one.

    b. the nickel-cadmium one.

    c. the lead-acid one.

    d. the environment-unfriendly one.

3. The oldest member of these Nobel Prize winners is

    a. M. Stanley Whittingham.

    b. Akira Yoshino.

    c. John B. Goodenough.

    d. unknown to us because their ages are not given in the article.

4. Lithium-ion is the

    a. most comfortable battery.

    b. bulkiest battery.

    c. lightest battery.

    d. oldest battery.

5. The lithium battery first became commercial in

    a. the 1970s.

    b. the 1980s.

    c. the 1990s.

    d. the early 2000s.

True or False

本文の内容に合致するものに T（True）、合致しないものに F（False）をつけなさい。

(   ) **1.** Dr. Goodenough is still active in his research.

(   ) **2.** The invention of Nickel-cadmium batteries transformed portable electronics.

(   ) **3.** iPhones are powered by lithium-ion batteries.

(   ) **4.** Even the scientists who won the Nobel Prize were amazed at the many adaptations of the lithium-ion battery.

(   ) **5.** In the early 1970s the world was not dependent on fossil fuels.

Vocabulary

次の英文は、読売新聞の The Japan News「えいご工房」に掲載された *Nobel awarded for developing battery*『電池開発にノーベル賞授与』の記事の一部です。下の語群から最も適切なものを1つ選び、(   )内に記入しなさい。

"Looking 10 years ahead and solving problems is how new technologies are developed," Yoshino said. This strong resolve was the (   ) for his innovation.

Soon after Yoshino joined Asahi Kasei in 1972, he spent all his time conducting research (   ) at finding new uses for chemical compounds. He came up with various (   ), such as a film that would make glass harder to break and insulating materials that would not (   ) burn, but none led to a commercialized product.

A turning point came in the 10th year of Yoshino's steady research. He started (   ) whether polyacetylene, a polymer with high conductivity (   ) by Hideki Shirakawa, professor emeritus at the University of Tsukuba, who won the 2000 Nobel Prize in Chemistry, could be used as a material for batteries. This (   ) idea led to the development of a special carbon material that enabled batteries to be much (   ).

aimed	considering	discovered	easily
ideas	impetus	novel	smaller

Unit 13

- ●フィンランドで世界最年少首相が誕生
- ●フィンランド、「世界で最も幸せな国」の王座維持

政治指導者中、女性の割合が多いフィンランドの世界最年少現役首相
のサンナ・マリン氏　　　　　　　　　　　Photo: 新華社／アフロ

Before you read

Republic of Finland
フィンランド共和国

面積　338,000km^2（日本よりやや小さい）
　　　　　　　　　　　　（世界64位）
人口　5,532,000人（世界116位）
首都　ヘルシンキ
言語　フィンランド語
　　　（全人口の5.2%スウェーデン語）
識字率　99%
民族　フィン人　91.7%
　　　スウェーデン人　5.5%
宗教　キリスト教・福音ルーテル派　78%
　　　キリスト教・フィンランド正教会　1.1%
　　　無宗教　20%
GDP　2,742億ドル（世界44位）
　　　1人当たりGDP　49,738ドル（世界15位）
通貨　ユーロ
政体　共和制

次の１～５の語句の説明として最も近いものをａ～ｅから１つ選び、（　　）内に記入しなさい。

1. sitting   (　　)   **a.** favoring social equality
2. at the helm   (　　)   **b.** essential
3. left-leaning   (　　)   **c.** believed or felt to exist
4. indispensable   (　　)   **d.** active or in office
5. perceived   (　　)   **e.** leading

Summary

次の英文は記事の要約です。下の語群から最も適切な語を１つ選び、（　　）内に記入しなさい。

1-74

    Finland continues to be (　　　　　　) as the world's happiest country. A comprehensive (　　　　　　) system, high levels of trust and effective democratic institutions appear to explain national (　　　　　　). So perhaps it is not (　　　　　　) that the new prime minister, the world's youngest, is a woman who places (　　　　　　) on public trust and extensive social welfare.

| contentment | importance | rated | surprising | welfare |

　「フィン人」の国フィンランドはスウェーデンの一部だったが、1809年にスウェーデンによりロシアに割譲された。1917年にはロシアから独立し、フィンランド共和国が成立した。

　独立後の政情や国際情勢は不安定だった。1939年からの２年間のソ連との冬戦争で国土の10分の１を失った。1941年から44年までソ連と対抗してドイツとイタリアと共に戦ったが、1944年にソ連と休戦し、国内駐留のドイツ軍を駆逐した。このため、バルト三国や東欧諸国のようにソ連に併合されたり、衛星国化されたりすることもなく、現在に至っている。

　GDP に対し、社会保障費が30.9％も占めている。徴兵制度があり、18歳以上の男子が対象だが、女子は志願制である。EU 志向外交を取っているが、ロシアとの間では良好な実務関係の発展に努めている。GDP と人口の規模は北海道とほぼ同じだが、1980年代以降、農業・林業中心からハイテク産業を基幹とする工業先進国へと著しい変化を遂げた。ノキアは有名である。

　2019年４月の総選挙で社会民主党が第１党となり、12月サンナ・マリン運輸通信大臣がフィンランド史上最年少の34歳で新首相に就任した。マリンは、両親の離婚後、母親とその同性パートナーに育てられた。

1-75

Sanna Marin of Finland to Become World's Youngest Prime Minister

> At 34, Ms. Marin will head a coalition made up of five parties, in a government led by women.

to Become：《大見出しで to 不定詞は未来を表す》

coalition：連立、連合

HELSINKI, Finland — Sanna Marin, 34, is set to become the world's youngest sitting prime minister when she is sworn in this week in Finland, after being elected to the position by her party late Sunday.

sitting prime minister：現職の首相

is sworn：宣誓する

position：（党首）の地位

5　The country's coalition government consists of five parties, four of which are led by women, with Ms. Marin now at the helm.　Four of the women are under the age of 35, which Finnish political experts say is more significant, symbolic of the rise of a new generation of politicians in the Nordic nation,
10　which has had strong female representation for decades.

at the helm：指揮する

Nordic：北欧の

representation：代議士、代表

1-76

Once sworn in, she will be Finland's youngest prime minister to date and its third female prime minister.

Ms. Marin, a left-leaning liberal, has been a member of Parliament since 2015.　She began her political career in 2012,
15　when she was elected to the local council in the southern city of Tampere.

left-leaning liberal：左派系自由主義者

local council：地方議会議員

Serving as Mr. Rinne's deputy when he took an extended sick leave earlier this year, she helped lead their party to a narrow win in national elections.

deputy：代理

extended sick leave：長期の病気休暇

national elections：国政選挙

1-77
20　"I have not actually ever thought about my age or my gender," she said, according to the national news outlet YLE. "I think of the reasons I got into politics and those things for which we have won the trust of the electorate."

YLE：フィンランド国営放送

electorate：選挙民

She noted that she had benefited from the welfare state
25　throughout her life, especially during "difficult times" and said that ensuring its strength was a priority for her.

welfare state：福祉国家

ensuring ～：～を確保する

priority：優先事項

"I got to live a safe childhood, have an education and pursue my dreams," she wrote. "Enabling it for everyone has driven me into politics."

got to ～：～できる機会を得た

　The New York Times, December 9, 2019

1-78

Finland retains crown as world's happiest country

Finland has once again been crowned as the world's happiest country, extending its lead over Denmark and Switzerland, according to a United Nations-affiliated research
35 network.

Finnish contentment stems from high levels of trust, which also underpins solid rankings across the rest of the Nordic region, the Sustainable Development Solutions Network said in the World Happiness Report on Friday.

40 Reliable and extensive welfare benefits, low corruption, and well-functioning democracy and state institutions are also key, as are a high sense of autonomy and freedom reported by their citizens.

1-79

"The World Happiness Report has proven to be an
45 indispensable tool for policymakers looking to better understand what makes people happy," said Jeffrey Sachs, director of the network.

The results are based on an average of three years of surveys between 2017 and 2019, meaning there's overlap
50 in the data from previous years, and include factors such as gross domestic product, social support from friends and family, healthy life expectancy, freedom to make life choices, generosity, perceived corruption and recent emotions — both happy and sad.

55 Afghanistan ranked lowest among 153 countries, with South Sudan and Zimbabwe just above it. The ranking saw the U.S. rise one place, to 18th.

The Japan Times based on Bloomberg, March 21, 2020

United Nations-affiliated research network：国連関連の研究ネットワーク

contentment：満足度

stems from 〜：〜から生じる

underpins 〜：〜を支える

Sustainable Development Solutions Network：持続可能な開発ソリューション・ネットワーク

World Happiness Report：世界幸福度報告

state institutions：国家機関

as 〜：〜と同じように《接続詞》

autonomy：自治

policymakers：政策立案者

looking to 〜：〜に関心を向ける

overlap：重複

healthy life expectancy：健康寿命

make life choices：人生の選択をする

perceived corruption：社会の腐敗度

saw the U.S. rise：《知覚動詞＋目的語＋原形不定詞》

Exercises

次の 1 ～ 5 の英文を完成させるために、 a ～ d の中から最も適切なものを 1 つ選びなさい。

1. The happiest country now is
    a. Denmark.
    b. Sweden.
    c. Finland.
    d. Switzerland.

2. One quality emphasized as an important factor in happiness is
    a. a Scandinavian diet.
    b. a cold climate.
    c. a high percentage of female politicians.
    d. sufficient social trust.

3. The least happy country on the list was
    a. The United States.
    b. Sudan.
    c. Afghanistan.
    d. Iraq.

4. Ms. Marin has the honor of being
    a. the second female Prime Minister in Finland.
    b. the youngest Prime Minister in Finland.
    c. from a wealthy family in Finland.
    d. the only female in the Finnish government.

5. A younger and more female tendency is reported
    a. in Finland's government.
    b. among Finland's right-wing parliamentarians.
    c. as the aging population retires.
    d. in Finland's opposition parties.

本文の内容に合致するものにT（True）、合致しないものにF（False）をつけなさい。

(   ) **1.** Ms. Marin is a right-leaning conservative who has also served in Parliament.

(   ) **2.** Ms. Marin tried to lead the party to win in the national elections as Mr. Rinne's deputy was unsuccessful.

(   ) **3.** Ms. Marin is in politics to enable others to have a safe childhood, a good education, and an opportunity to follow one's dreams.

(   ) **4.** Four of five coalition parties are led by men in Finland.

(   ) **5.** Finland is known to possess extensive welfare benefits, low corruption, and a well- functioning democracy.

Vocabulary

次の1〜8は、「happy」に関する英文です。日本文に合わせて（   ）内に、必要があれば happy を適当な形に直して記入しなさい。

1. 一生懸命勉強するか、全くしないかではなく、中間を取ろう。
I try to strike a (   ) medium between studying too hard and not studying at all.

2. その映画はハッピーエンドだ。
The film ends (   ).

3. 幸福は買えない。
You cannot buy (   ).

4. これほど幸福なことはない。
I have never been (   ).

5. ちっとも幸福ではない。
I am far from (   ).

6. 世界で一番幸福者だ。
I am the (   ) person in the world.

7. 喜んで参加しましょう。
I will (   ) take part.

8. 健康は幸福に欠くことができない。
Health is essential to (   ).

●サウジ社会の変化はコーヒーハウスを覗けば分かる

イスラム教国サウジアラビアが変わりつつある。首都リヤドにあるコーヒーハウスの店内
風景

Photo: The New York Times ／ Redux ／アフロ

Before you read

Kingdom of Saudi Arabia
サウジアラビア王国

面積　2,150,000km²（日本の約5.7倍）（世界12位）
人口　34,269,000人（世界41位）
首都　リヤド
公用語　アラビア語
民族　サウジアラビア人　73％
　　　ヨーロッパ系　1％以下
　　　アラブ系　6％ ／アフリカ系　1％
　　　アジア系　20％
宗教　イスラム教スンニ派　85〜90％
　　　　　　　　シーア派　10〜15％
GDP　7,865億ドル（世界18位）
　　　1人当たり GDP　23,539ドル　（世界40位）
通貨　サウジアラビア・リヤル
政体　君主制
識字率　94.8％

次の1〜5の語句の説明として最も近いものをa〜eから1つ選び、（　　）内に記入しなさい。

1. on the front line 　　（　　）　　**a.** soaked

2. head-spinning 　　（　　）　　**b.** fast-changing and surprising

3. segregate 　　（　　）　　**c.** separate

4. skew 　　（　　）　　**d.** lean disproportionately toward

5. infused 　　（　　）　　**e.** at the leading edge

Summary

次の英文は記事の要約です。下の語群から最も適切な語を1つ選び、（　　）内に記入しなさい。

2-01

　Saudi society is changing fast, with cafes (　　　　　　) this most clearly. Until recently, men and women had to be separated in (　　　　　) places, but in many cafes both sexes are now (　　　　　). In more (　　　　　) cities like Jeddah young women can be seen chatting in cafes without head scarves. Some are (　　　　　) working as baristas.

even	liberal	mixing	public	showing

　　サウジアラビアは、ベネズエラに次ぐ世界2位の石油埋蔵量・生産量・輸出量を誇るエネルギー大国である。輸出総額の約9割、財政収入の約8割を石油に依存している。さらに、OPEC石油輸出国機構の指導国として国際石油市場に強い影響力を有している。

　　イスラム教最大の聖地メッカと第2のメディナの二大聖地を擁するイスラム世界の中心的存在で、主導的役割を果たしている。しかし、2014年以降原油価格低迷で財政赤字に陥り、18年には付加価値税を導入し、財源確保に努めて来た。

　　2016年12月、初めて女性の選挙権・被選挙権が認められ、女性20名が当選した。さらに社会・経済改革計画「ビジョン2030」を発表し、文化や娯楽活動、スポーツの振興、女性の社会進出促進、製造業や観光業の振興を掲げた。サウジ人労働力の積極的利用、石油部門以外の発展に力を注ぎ、人材育成・民営化・外資導入・市場開放など諸改革に努めている。

　　2017年6月にサルマン国王の3番目の妻との間の副皇太子ムハンマドを皇太子に昇格した。皇太子は脱石油依存の経済改革を主導し、2019年12月11日、国営石油会社サウジアラムコを証券取引所タダウルに株式を上場した。上場時の株式時価総額は約1兆8800億ドルとなり、世界最大の上場会社となった。

Reading

2-02

Saudi Society Is Changing.
Just Take a Look at These Coffeehouses.

As the government relaxes restrictions on men and women working and socializing together, coffeehouses are on the front lines of change.

RIYADH, Saudi Arabia — For insight into these head-spinning times in Saudi Arabia, where the ultraconservative social and religious codes that micromanage daily life seem to spring a new leak every month — women driving! movie
5 theaters! Usher and Akon rapping to sold-out crowds! — it sometimes pays to read the Google Maps reviews of specialty coffee shops.

2-03

"I visited this place and was in a total shock!" Tarak Alhamood, a customer at Nabt Fenjan, a Riyadh coffee shop,
10 raged online recently. "You're violating the rules of this country. I hope this place gets closed permanently."

The issue was the decision that made Nabt Fenjan a daring outpost of the new Riyadh: Originally opened only for women, the coffee shop began allowing male and female customers to
15 mix in late 2018.

The move propelled the cafe ahead of the law in the kingdom, where most restaurants and coffee shops are divided, by law and custom, into all-male "singles" sections and "family" sections for women and mixed family groups.
20 Men enter through separate doors and pay in separate lines; women sometimes eat behind partitions to ensure privacy from male strangers.

2-04

In early December, however, the government announced that businesses would no longer be required to segregate
25 customers — the latest expansion of the social reforms initiated by the de facto Saudi ruler, Crown Prince Mohammed bin Salman.

Some women whose families might previously have

insight into ～：～への洞察

head-spinning：頭がくらくらする

codes：規範

spring a new leak：新たに漏れ出る

Usher and Akon：～アッシャーとエイコン《共に米国人歌手》

sold-out crowds：チケット売り切れのコンサート会場に集まった大勢の人

pays：良い、得になる

specialty coffee shops：コーヒー専門店

daring outpost：向こう見ずな前哨基地

move：行動、戦略

strangers：見知らぬ人

segregate ～：～を分離する

de facto：事実上の

Crown Prince：皇太子

allowed them to work only in the privacy of offices, if at
30 all, now hold barista jobs. Saudis can now mingle with the
opposite sex not only at home but also at movie theaters,
concerts and even wrestling matches. Young entrepreneurs
are opening places where Saudis can meet like-minded
people of both sexes, whether they are artists, filmmakers or
35 entrepreneurs.

2-05

    The clientele in such coffee shops skews young, reflecting a
country where more than two-thirds of the population is under
30 and an unknown proportion is chronically bored. Bars are
barred, concerts and movies just starting to become widely
40 available. Evenings out, therefore, still tend to revolve around
food and (nonalcoholic) drink, the more Instagrammable, the
better.

    Most coffee shops are still gender-segregated. But many
have other draws: imported Japanese brewing equipment,
45 Instagrammable tarts and — more intangible, but mandatory
nevertheless — good vibes.

2-06

    Virtually none offer the golden, cardamom-infused Arabic
coffee, poured from a curvaceous pot into dainty cups and
served to guests with a hillock of dates, that traditionally
50 defined Saudi coffee culture.

    Instead, at Draft, which still separates single men and
"families," there are quinoa salads and blond-wood tables
illuminated by industrial-style bulbs. And Medd Café in
Jeddah, the Red Sea city where social codes have long been
55 more relaxed than elsewhere, the organic, fair-trade beans are
roasted in-house.

    On a recent Friday night at Medd Café, the outdoor patio
was crowded with young men and women. Many of the
women wore their hair uncovered and their abayas open over
60 jeans and sneakers, styling them more like long, fluid jackets
than the traditional all-covering gowns.

The New York Times, January 15, 2020

in the privacy of 〜：〜で
こっそりと

if at all：仮にあったとし
ても

barista：バリスタ《カフェ
でエスプレッソコーヒー
をつくる専門職人》

like-minded：同じ考えを持
った、同好の

clientele：常連客

skews young：若い人たち
に偏る

bored：退屈している

barred：禁じられている《イ
スラム教では飲酒は禁止》

revolve around 〜：〜を中
心に展開する

Instagrammable：インスタ
映えする

draws：魅力あるもの、人
を引き付けるもの

brewing equipment：エス
プレッソマシン、抽出機

intangible：触れることの
できない

vibes：雰囲気

cardamom-infused 〜：〜
カルダモン（香辛料）入
りの

dainty：小ぶりの

dates：ナツメヤシの実

quinoa：キノア《雑穀の一種》

blond-wood：ブロンド・ウ
ッド製の《blond wood；ブ
ロンド色の木材》

industrial-style bulbs：産
業用電球

fair-trade：フェアトレード
《農産物を買う際に、生産
者が適切な収入を得られ
るように適正価格を支払
う運動》

patio：中庭

abayas：アバヤ《アラビア
半島の女性の全身を覆う
伝統的衣装》

styling 〜：〜を着こなす

fluid：優雅な、流麗な

Exercises

　次の１〜３の英文を完成させ、４〜５の英文の質問に答えるために、ａ〜ｄの中から最も適切なものを１つ選びなさい。

1. The old rules when Nabt Fenjan first opened were that

　　a. men and women customers had to sit separately.

　　b. men had to enter through separate doors.

　　c. women sometimes were required to eat behind partitions, out of view of the men.

　　d. men were not allowed in the café.

2. Women are surprisingly allowed to

　　a. stay home and not go into business.

　　b. become baristas in coffee shops.

　　c. drink alcohol.

　　d. take care of their family.

3. Artists, filmmakers and entrepreneurs are described as

　　a. concealing their creative activities from others.

　　b. enjoying quinoa salads while conversing with other creative people.

　　c. increasingly able to meet with individuals who have similar interests.

　　d. unable to benefit from the changes in Saudi Arabia.

4. What percentage of the population in Saudi Arabia are under 30 years old?

　　a. Under 6%.

　　b. Around 30%.

　　c. About 33%.

　　d. Over 66%.

5. What do traditional coffee shop offer customers?

　　a. Organic fair-trade fresh roasted beans.

　　b. Quinoa salads.

　　c. Arabic coffee and dates.

　　d. Cappuccino coffee.

本文の内容に合致するものに T（True）、合致しないものに F（False）をつけなさい。

(   ) **1.** Women are now allowed to drive a car.

(   ) **2.** Usher and Akon were not allowed to perform in Saudi Arabia.

(   ) **3.** Most coffee shops are still gender-segregated.

(   ) **4.** Crown Prince Mohammad bin Salman is largely responsible for the social reform in Saudi Arabia.

(   ) **5.** Tables in coffee shops are not allowed to have industrial-style bulbs.

Vocabulary

次の英文は、The New York Times に掲載された *Aramco Sets I.P.O. Target: $25.6 Billion*『アラムコ、新規公開株 I.P.O ２兆56億ドル上場』の記事の一部です。下の語群から最も適切なものを１つ選び、（   ）内に記入しなさい。

Saudi Arabia's giant state-(   ) oil company, Saudi Aramco, on Thursday set the price of its initial public offering at a level that would raise $25.6 billion, a sum that is expected to make it the world's (   ) I.P.O.

The I.P.O. will establish Aramco as one of the world's most (   ) companies, but the $1.7 trillion figure falls (   ) of the Saudi royal family's hopes of an offering that valued the company at close to $2 trillion.

Global investors proved to be (   ) over the earlier valuations offered by the Saudi government. While its filings showed Aramco to be immensely profitable – it posted a profit of $68 billion for the first nine months of the year – its earnings have declined, and risks like global (   ) and geopolitical instability cast a pall over its prospects.

The I.P.O. process has been agonizingly slow since Crown Prince Mohammed bin Salman, Saudi Arabia's de facto ruler, first raised the idea of making the crown (   ) of the Saudi economy a public company more than two years ago.

After big early promises, the Saudis have taken a more cautious approach, restricting the listing initially to Saudi Arabia in order to (   ) the more rigorous disclosures that would be required in New York or London.

avoid	biggest	jewel	owned
short	skittish	valuable	warming

●移民流入は壁では阻止できない

米国カリフォルニア州シリコンバレーのサニーベールにあるインド服飾専門店

Before you read

United States of America
アメリカ合衆国

面積　9,628,000km²（日本の約25.5倍）（世界３位）
人口　327,750,000人（世界３位）
首都　ワシントンDC
最大都市　ニューヨーク
公用語　なし、事実上は英語
識字率　93.5%
人種　白人　72.4% ／ ヒスパニック　18.5%
　　　黒人　12.7% ／ アジア系　4.8%
　　　ネイティブアメリカン　0.9%
宗教　キリスト教・カトリック　20%
　　　キリスト教・プロテスタント　57%
　　　ユダヤ教　1.3%
　　　イスラム教　0.9%
　　　無宗教　20.8%
GDP　20兆5802億ドル（世界１位）
　　　１人当たりGDP　62,869ドル（世界９位）
通貨　USドル
政体　大統領制・連邦制

次の１〜５の語の説明として最も近いものをａ〜ｅから１つ選び、（　）内に記入しなさい。

1. deter	（　）	**a.**	walk through water
2. undocumented	（　）	**b.**	heavily
3. round-around	（　）	**c.**	dissuade
4. wade	（　）	**d.**	long and complicated route
5. overwhelmingly	（　）	**e.**	without legal papers or permission

Summary

次の英文は記事の要約です。下の語群から最も適切な語を１つ選び、（　）内に記入しなさい。

Since Trump became president, discussion about (　　　　) immigration has focused on the (　　　　) border with Mexico. But almost half America's undocumented residents entered by air and (　　　　) immigration checks. They only became illegal when they (　　　　) to return on time. Officials have been (　　　　) to keep track of all of the thousands who simply decide to stay.

> completed　　failed　　illegal　　land　　unable

　　アメリカが迎い入れた移民の数は、世界のどの国よりも多く、5,000万人を超えている。Trump 政権になっても年間70万人近い移民を受け入れている。1990年のアメリカの人口のうち2,000万人は、外国生まれだった。ニューヨーク湾内のエリス島にある自由の女神像の台座にエマ・ラザルスの詩の一節「疲れし者、貧しき者を我に与えよ。自由の空気を吸わんと熱望する人たちよ…、身を寄せ合う哀れな人たちよ。住む家なく、嵐にもまれし者を我に送りたまえ。我は、黄金の扉にて灯を掲げん」が刻まれている。アメリカは、ヨーロッパ諸国からやって来た移民たちに自由と希望を与えた黄金の扉だった。

　　しかし、1619年から1808年までの間、強制的に奴隷として連れて来られた50万人のアフリカ人もいる。今日アフリカ系アメリカ人は、総人口の12.7％を占めている。さらに、スペイン語圏の出身者ヒスパニック系の移民も1970年代から急増し、今日約2,700万人もいる。５割はメキシコ系である。また、今日、アジア系アメリカ人が約1,000万人いるが、最も成功度の高い移民グループだ。今日約500万人の不法滞在者がいて、年間27万5,000人の割合で増え、社会福祉制度に大きな負担となっている。1986年に移民法が改正され、90万人が合法的に滞在する資格を得た。

Reading

2-08

An Immigrant Influx That a Wall Won't Deter

Immigrant Influx：移民の流入

Deter ～：～を阻止する

> Millions Who Legally Enter the United States
> As Students or Tourists Never Go Back

SUNNYVALE, Calif.—Eddie Oh, an industrial engineer, lost his job during the financial crisis that gripped South Korea in 1998. With no prospects, he scrounged together his savings to pay his family's airfare to California. They were
5 going on vacation, he told the United States embassy, which issued six-month visitor visas for the family.

financial crisis：金融危機

With no prospects：見込みはない

They ～ vacation：《told の直接目的語》

visitor visas：観光ビザ

2-09

The Ohs headed to Sunnyvale, a middle-class community in California's Silicon Valley where a relative already had rented a small apartment. The Ohs moved in, nine people
10 crammed into two rooms. Mr. Oh got to work painting houses. His wife found a job as a waitress. And their children, Eli, 11, and Sue, 9, started school.

"We were constantly in debt. We struggled to pay the rent," said Eli Oh, who grew up to be a critical-care response
15 nurse at Stanford University. "Nobody ever thought we were illegally here, because we didn't fit the stereotype."

in debt：借金している

critical-care response nurse：救命救急対応看護師

stereotype：固定観念、イメージ

2-10

They are hardly alone. Though President Trump has staked much of his presidency on halting the movement of undocumented immigrants across the southern border, the Oh
20 family's round-around route to residence in the United States is part of one of America's least widely known immigration stories.

undocumented：ビザや ID のない

least ～：ほとんど～でない

Some 350,000 travelers arrive by air in the United States each day. From Asia, South America and Africa, they come
25 mostly with visas allowing them to tour, study, do business or attend a conference for an authorized period of time.

authorized：認定された

Nearly half of the estimated 11 million undocumented immigrants now in the country did not trek through the desert or wade across the Rio Grande to enter the country; they flew
30 in with a visa, passed inspection at the airport—and stayed.

inspection：審査

2-11

Many undocumented Asians—including a large number from India—have settled like the Ohs in and around Sunnyvale, about 50 miles southeast of San Francisco, according to the Center for Migration Studies analysis.

35   Apple, LinkedIn and other tech titans in the area employ many whom the companies have sponsored for legal work visas or permanent residency in the United States.

Some of them stay on as independent programming contractors after their visas have expired or after leaving a
40 company that sponsored them for a visa.

But developing policies to curb overstays requires accurate data, experts say, and Homeland Security officials still lack a reliable system to track them.

2-12

Most travelers are photographed and fingerprinted at
45 American consulates abroad when they receive a visa and then again on arrival in the United States. But Customs and Border Protection still depends overwhelmingly on biographical information from the manifests of departing travelers, provided by airlines, to tally who did not leave in
50 time, or at all.

Immigration and Customs Enforcement, which enforces immigration rules in the interior of the country, said that it puts a priority on identifying those who pose potential national security or public-safety threats. In fiscal 2018, its Homeland
55 Security Investigations unit made 1,808 arrests in connection with visa-violation leads.

The New York Times, December 2, 2019

settled in 〜：〜に住み着く

Center for Migration
  Studies：移民研究センタ
  ー《ニューヨークを本拠
  とするシンクタンク》
LinkedIn：リンクトイン
  《世界最大級のビジネス型
  SNS; 親会社はマイクロソ
  フト》
permanent residency：永住
  権

contractors：請負（受託）
  業者

expired：有効期限が切れた

curb overstays：ビザが切れ
  た不法滞在者を抑制する
Homeland Security：国土安
  全保障省《各国の内務省
  に相当》
consulates：領事館

Customs and Border
  Protection：税関・国境
  取締局《国土安全保障省
  の一部門》
biographical
  information：略歴

manifests：乗客名簿

tally 〜：〜を記録する

Immigration and Customs
  Enforcement：移民・関
  税執行局《国土安全保障
  省の一部門》
immigration rules：入国管
  理法令
identifying 〜：〜を割り
  出す
pose potential threats：脅
  威をもたらしかねない

fiscal：会計年度

Homeland Security
  Investigations unit：米国
  の安全に関する捜査部

visa-violation leads：不正
  ビザの「おとり捜査」

Exercises

Multiple Choice

次の１の英文の質問に答え、２〜５の英文を完成させるために、ａ〜ｄの中から最も適切なものを１つ選びなさい。

1. At the time of writing, about how many people flew into the U.S. each day?

    a. 3,500.
    b. 50,000.
    c. 300,000.
    d. 350,000.

2. The Oh family entered the U.S.

    a. illegally.
    b. with legal visas.
    c. fitting the popular stereotype of immigrants.
    d. intending to return to South Korea.

3. Half of the immigrants in the U.S.

    a. trekked through the desert to get into the country.
    b. waded across the Rio Grande from Mexico.
    c. flew in legally as tourists and overstayed their visas.
    d. climbed the border fence in order to get in.

4. Sunnyvale, California is known for

    a. high tech companies like Apple.
    b. offering many job opportunities.
    c. its peaceful middle-class community.
    d. all of the above features.

5. The author feels that President Trump's beloved wall

    a. will mostly solve the problem of immigration "overstays."
    b. will be far too expensive to be completed.
    c. has managed to reduce illegal immigration to a large degree.
    d. is irrelevant to the way many illegal immigrants enter the U.S.

本文の内容に合致するものに T（True）、合致しないものに F（False）をつけなさい。

(　　) **1.** Eli Oh became a critical care nurse at Stanford.

(　　) **2.** There are currently 6 million undocumented immigrants in the U.S.

(　　) **3.** The Ohs' first jobs helped them get started and established in their new country.

(　　) **4.** Apple, LinkedIn and other tech companies sometimes sponsor employees for permanent residency in the U.S.

(　　) **5.** The U.S. Embassy never issues 6-month visas.

Vocabulary

次の英文は、Pew Research Center の Fact Tank News in the Numbers: *Key findings about U.S. immigrants*『アメリカの移民に関する主な調査結果』の一部です。下の語群から最も適切なものを１つ選び、（　　　）内に記入しなさい。

The United States has (　　　　) immigrants than any other country in the world. Today, more than 40 million people living in the U.S. were born in (　　　　) country, accounting for about one-fifth of the world's (　　　　) in 2017. The population of immigrants is also very (　　　　), with just about every country in the world represented among U.S. immigrants.

Most immigrants (77%) are in the country (　　　　), while almost a quarter are unauthorized. In 2017, 45% were naturalized U.S. citizens. Some 27% of immigrants were permanent residents and 5% were (　　　　) residents in 2017.

The decline in the unauthorized immigrant population is due largely to a (　　　　) in the number from Mexico. Meanwhile, there was a rise in the number from Central America and Asia.

Generally, most immigrants eligible for naturalization apply to become citizens. However, Mexican lawful immigrants have the lowest naturalization rate overall. (　　　　) and personal barriers, lack of interest and financial barriers are the top reasons for choosing not to naturalize cited by Mexican-born green card holders.

another	diverse	fall	language
legally	migrants	more	temporary

●ギリシャの難民秘密収容所では「まるで動物扱い」

難民として認められずにギリシャの国境警備隊によりトルコに強制送還されたシリア人たち

Photo: The New York Times ／ Redux ／アフロ

Before you read

Hellenic Republic（Greece）
ギリシャ共和国

面積　131,957km²（日本の約３分の１）（世界95位）
人口　10,473,000人（世界87位）
首都　アテネ
公用語　現代ギリシャ語
民族　ギリシャ人　98%
　　　アルメニア人　／ アルバニア人　／ トルコ系
　　　ユダヤ系
宗教　ギリシャ正教
GDP　2,182億ユーロ（世界52位）
　　　１人当たり GDP　20,317ユーロ（世界44位）
通貨　ユーロ
識字率　97.9%
政体　共和制

次の１〜５の語の説明として最も近いものを a 〜 e から１つ選び、（　　）内に記入しなさい。

1. detain 　　（　　）　**a.** take property for legal reasons
2. expel 　　（　　）　**b.** arrest
3. refoulement （　　）　**c.** sending refugees somewhere that may be unsafe
4. dismantle 　（　　）　**d.** send away
5. confiscate 　（　　）　**e.** take apart or knock down

Summary

　次の英文は記事の要約です。下の語群から最も適切な語を１つ選び、（　　）内に記入しなさい。

2-13

　　In 2015 Europe received a huge number of (　　　　　　), many of them entering through Greece. Nowadays European governments are (　　　　　　) to accept more asylum-seekers, and the Greeks feel under (　　　　　) to keep out all the people being pushed in their (　　　　　) by Turkey. Journalists are confirming reports of violence and even killings by the (　　　　　).

authorities 　　 direction 　　 pressure 　　 refugees 　　 reluctant

　2020年２月29日トルコのエルドアン大統領が、国内にとどまる移民のヨーロッパに向けた出国を容認することを宣言した。これを受け、トルコに滞在している難民らがギリシャとの国境沿いに殺到した。ギリシャ側は国境警備に1,200人の軍要員を増強し、国境フェンスの約30km 延長も決め、流入を阻止した。しかし島しょ部では、難民がトルコ経由で押し寄せ、滞在施設の収容人数も大きく超え、劣悪な環境問題になっている。

　さらに、ギリシャは「ヨーロッパの盾」として国境管理のため、７億ユーロの緊急支援を決め、水際対策強化を示した。ギリシャは財政再建のために、2015年８月、EU から2,566億ユーロの融資を受けている。2060年の期限までに、75％の債務を返済しなければならない。しかし、トルコとギリシャの国境での難民受け入れ、阻止に関する紛争も2019年11月末に発生した新型コロナウイルスの流行で、薄れて来ている。

　2020年８月トルコの新型コロナウイルス感染者数は23.8万人、ギリシャは5,270人。両国とも渡航中止を勧告している。しかし、ギリシャ南西部のポルトヘリのホテルに収容されているカメルーンやコンゴ民主共和国からの150名の難民申請者が、新型コロナウイルスに感染したと発表された。彼らと集団生活をおくっていた471人全員が隔離され、町全体にも15日間の移動制限がかけられた。

Reading

2-14

'We Are Like Animals' : Inside Greece's Secret Site for Migrants

> The extrajudicial center is one of several tactics Greece is using to prevent a repeat of the 2015 migration crisis.

    POROS, Greece — The Greek government is detaining migrants incommunicado at a secret extrajudicial location before expelling them to Turkey without due process, one of several hard-line measures taken to seal its borders to Europe
5 that experts say violate international law.

2-15

    Several migrants said in interviews that they had been captured, stripped of their belongings, beaten and expelled from Greece without being given a chance to claim asylum or speak to a lawyer, in an illegal process known as refoulement.
10 Meanwhile, Turkish officials said that at least three migrants had been shot and killed while trying to enter Greece in the past two weeks.

    The Greek approach is the starkest example of European efforts to prevent a reprise of the 2015 migration crisis in
15 which more than 850,000 undocumented people passed relatively easily through Greece to other parts of Europe, roiling the Continent's politics and fueling the rise of the far right.

2-16

    If thousands more refugees reach Greece, Greek officials
20 fear being left to care for them for years, with little support from other members in the European Union, exacerbating social tensions and further fraying a strained economy.

    The Greek government has defended its actions as a legitimate response to recent provocations by the Turkish
25 authorities, who have transported thousands of migrants to the Greek-Turkish border since late February and have encouraged some to charge and dismantle a border fence.

    The Greek authorities have denied reports of deaths along

---

Site for Migrants：難民収容所

extrajudicial center：超法規的な施設

POROS：ポロス島《エーゲ海に浮かぶ島》

detaining ～：～を拘留する

expelling ～ to …：～を…へ追放する

due process：法的な手続き

seal ～：～を封鎖する

stripped of ～：～を剝奪される

asylum：亡命

refoulement：ルフールマン、追放・送還《難民条約に、追放・送還禁止条項がある》

reprise：再現

undocumented：密（不法）入国の

roiling ～：～を混乱させる

rise of the far right：極右勢力の台頭

left to ～．～するよう任せられる

exacerbating ～：～をさらに悪化させる

fraying ～：～をボロボロにする

legitimate response to ～：～への正当な反応

provocations：挑発

charge and dismantle ～：～に体当たりして壊す

the border.

2-17
But through a combination of on-the-ground reporting and forensic analysis of satellite imagery, The Times has confirmed the existence of the secret center in northeastern Greece.

forensic analysis：科学捜査

Using footage supplied to several media outlets, The Times has also established that the Greek Coast Guard, nominally a lifesaving institution, fired shots in the direction of migrants onboard a dinghy that was trying to reach Greek shores early this month, beat them with sticks and sought to repel them by driving past them at high speed, risking tipping them into water.

footage：ビデオ映像

established ～：～を確証した

Coast Guard：沿岸警備隊

nominally：名目上は

dinghy：小型ボート

tipping ～ into water：～を海に落とす

Forensic analysis of videos provided by witnesses also confirmed the death of at least one person — a Syrian factory worker — after he was shot on the Greek-Turkish border.

2-18
Mr. al-Hussein, a trainee software engineer, who recently received a Turkish passport, went to the border to see if the way was clear for his family, who only have Syrian nationality. He spent that night in the rain on the bank of the Evros River, which divides western Turkey from eastern Greece. Early the next morning, he reached the Greek side in a rubber dinghy packed with other migrants.

see if ～：～かどうかを調べる

But his journey ended an hour later, he said in a recent interview. Captured by Greek border guards, he said, he and his group were taken to a detention site.

border guards：国境警備隊

detention site：拘留場所（施設）

His phone was confiscated to prevent him from making calls, he said, and his requests to claim asylum and contact United Nations officials were ignored.

confiscated：没収された

"To them, we are like animals," Mr. al-Hussein said of the Greek guards.

The New York Times, March 10, 2020

Multiple Choice

次の１〜４の英文を完成させ、５の英文の質問に答えるために、ａ〜ｄの中から最も適切なものを１つ選びなさい。

1. Greece is thought to be violating international law by

    a. preventing migrants from escaping to Turkey.

    b. moving migrants to a secret location in Syria.

    c. forcing migrants to enter the E.U.

    d. sending refugees back to Turkey without allowing the due process.

2. The Greeks have closed their borders because

    a. they do not want a repeat of the 2015 migration crisis.

    b. Turkey made a hole in the border fence to enable migrants to enter Greece.

    c. they don't want their own citizens to see their poor treatment of migrants.

    d. of all of the above reasons.

3. According to this article, the Greeks have

    a. denied allegations of people dying on the border.

    b. held immigrants at secret centers.

    c. fired shots at any immigrants.

    d. done all of the above things.

4. The European Union is

    a. helping Greece to bear the cost of supporting and caring for immigrants.

    b. offering little assistance to the Greeks.

    c. expecting migrants to boost its economy.

    d. welcoming arrivals from Turkey but not from Syria.

5. How many migrants passed through Greece during the 2015 crisis?

    a. 8,500.

    b. 85,000.

    c. 580,000.

    d. 850,000.

本文の内容に合致するものに T（True）、合致しないものに F（False）をつけなさい。

( ) **1.** The migrants only want to stay in Greece.

( ) **2.** At least one person was killed by the Greek Coast Guard while trying to enter Greece.

( ) **3.** The United Nations has intervened and tried to rectify the problems in Greece.

( ) **4.** This article hints at the fact that there are poor relationships between Greece and Turkey.

( ) **5.** The Greeks feel that if the immigrants stay it will cause further problems for their unsteady economy.

Vocabulary

次の 1～8 は、移民や難民に関する英文です。下の語群から最も適切なものを 1 つ選び、( ) 内に記入しなさい。

1. An ( ) seeker wants protection and shelter in another country.
2. A ship of Italian ( ) left Naples for Australia.
3. Japan has more economic migrants than human rights ( ).
4. Australia was a British ( ) before becoming an independent country.
5. America's early European immigrants were helped by ( ) people.
6. Since the late 1970s, thousands of ( ) people have left Vietnam.
7. On arrival you should present your passport to the ( ) officer.
8. Those birds ( ) north in summer and south in winter.

asylum	boat	colony	emigrants
immigration	migrate	native	refugees

Unit 17

- 「桜戦士」、チームの結束を称賛
- 日本のファンは歴史的成果を褒めちぎる

ラグビー・ワールドカップ1次リーグでのスコットランドとの最終戦で勝利し喜ぶ「桜戦士」

Photo: Kyodo News

Before you read

次のa〜hのラグビーに該当するものを①〜⑧の中から選びなさい。

a. forward （　　） ① putting the ball into play at the start of the first or second half

b. half-time （　　） ② taking hold of a player and making them fall

c. linc-out （　　） ③ the interval between the two halves of the game

d. kickoff （　　） ④ a free kick

e. penalty kick （　　） ⑤ five points won by grounding the ball

f. scrum(mage) （　　） ⑥ the players pushing together with their heads down

g. tackle （　　） ⑦ restarting play by throwing the ball in from the sideline

h. try （　　） ⑧ player who competes for the ball in a scrum

次の１〜５の語句の説明として最も近いものを a〜e から１つ選び、(　　)内に記入しなさい。

1. make a run	(　　)	**a.**	say or do something similar
2. echo	(　　)	**b.**	able to
3. capable of	(　　)	**c.**	not quite reaching a goal
4. short of	(　　)	**d.**	act as organizer and inviter
5. host	(　　)	**e.**	progress through several rounds

次の英文は記事の要約です。下の語群から最も適切な語を１つ選び、(　　)内に記入しなさい。

2-19

Japan's squad (　　　　　　) the last eight at the Rugby World Cup on home territory. The Brave Blossoms (　　　　　) their previous performances. On the way they (　　　　　) Ireland and Scotland, two nations with long rugby traditions. Coach Jamie Joseph (　　　　　) the achievement to the players' hard work, while team member Michael Leitch also (　　　　　) the importance of unity.

---

attributed　　defeated　　exceeded　　made　　stressed

　　1823年イングランドのパブリックスクール・ラグビー校でフットボールの試合中に、William Web Ellis がボールを抱えたまま相手のゴール目指して走り出した。1840年にはボールを持って走る「running in」が確立、普及し出した。その当時、現代のサッカーは生まれておらず、Ellis が手でボールを扱ったことではなく、ボールを持って走った行為が、フットボールではルール違反だった。現在のラグビーは、13人制の rugby league と15人制の rugby union がある。日本のラグビーは通常 rugby union である。

　　2019年10月にラグビーワールドカップ日本大会が行われた。日本チーム「桜戦士」は開幕戦でロシアに快勝し、ワールドカップ優勝候補のアイルランドから歴史的金星を挙げた。続くサモア戦で４トライを奪って勝利し、強豪スコットランド戦では相手の猛攻に耐えてグループリーグ４連勝で１位通過し、初めて８強入りを果たし、日本中に熱狂をもたらした。準々決勝で南アフリカに敗れたものの、国籍や出身地を超えてチーム一丸となって戦う姿に日本中が熱狂し、「にわかファン」という造語も登場した。チームのスローガン「One Team ワンチーム」が2019年度の新語・流行語大賞に選ばれた。さらに6,464億円の経済波及効果をもたらした。

Reading

Brave Blossoms praise team unity

Japan coach Jamie Joseph said Monday the team's impressive work ethic played a major role in the hosts making a run to the Rugby World Cup's last eight for the first time.

Speaking a day after the Brave Blossoms were knocked
5 out of the tournament via a 26-3 defeat to South Africa, Joseph said "the team had worked incredibly hard for the last three years."

He also paid tribute to the players who did not make the World Cup squad, saying they "had contributed just as much."
10 Joseph's future with the national team remains in doubt due to difficulties that have arisen regarding his proposed contract extension, according to sources.

But no matter what happens next, he wanted to make sure he thanked the nation for their support and the players for
15 their belief in what he was trying to achieve.

Michael Leitch echoed his coach, saying the team's unity played a big role in their ability to go through the pool stages unbeaten, defeating two Tier One sides along the way.

"I'm proud to be the captain of this team," he said. "I'm
20 happy we made the best eight. The reason we got this far is because Jamie united us and made us one team."

Four years ago, the Japan Rugby Football Union failed to ride the momentum of Japan's success in England and the players spoke of their hope that this time around things would
25 be different.

"When we came back from New Zealand after the 2011 tournament, there were only two or three reporters, so it's unbelievable to see so many of you here today," hooker Shota Horie said of the news conference, which was broadcast live
30 on TV.

"It's our mission to work toward the next World Cup and keep up the popularity of rugby. What matters is how much

---

Brave Blossoms：「桜戦士」、ラグビー日本代表《胸のエンブレムが桜》

work ethic：労働意欲

hosts making a run to 〜：開催国の日本代表が〜まで一気に駆け上がったこと

last eight：ベスト8

via 〜：〜によって

defeat to 〜：〜に敗北

paid tribute to 〜：〜を称賛した

make the World Cup squad：ワールドカップに出場するチームに参加する

contract extension：契約延長

sources：消息筋

no matter what happens：何が起きようが

echoed 〜：〜に同調した

pool stages：予選リーグ

Tier One sides：一流チーム

Japan Rugby Football Union：日本ラグビー・フットボール協会《公益財団法人；日本におけるラグビーの高校・大学・ジャパンラグビートップリーグを総括する国内競技連盟》

momentum：勢い

success：活躍

this time around：今度は

hooker：フッカー《フォワード最前列中央のプレーヤー；スクラムの際、ボールを味方の方へかき出す》

Shota Horie：堀江翔太

What matters：大事なのは

stronger and better we can get from here on," Horie said.

Flyhalf Yu Tamura, who broke a rib during the defeat to
35 South Africa, said he had "realized through this tournament
that we're capable of doing our very best and becoming the
national team that everyone admires and wants to join."

Japanese fans laud historic effort

Japan fell a win short of making the final four at the Rugby
40 World Cup, but both those involved in the game and others
watching from the outside said Sunday they are proud of what
the team achieved.

"Watching them beat Ireland, then Scotland (in the pool
stages), it was more than I thought was possible. I want
45 Japan to keep improving and win the World Cup one day,"
Yokohama resident Musashi Oka said after watching Japan
lose its quarterfinal 26-3 to South Africa from a fan zone
outside Oita Station.

The 27-year-old, among hundreds of Japanese and foreign
50 fans in Oita, said meeting rugby fans from around the world
has been a highlight of the World Cup so far. "It's been so
much fun, I hope we can host it again," he said.

The Japan Times based on Kyodo, October 22, 2019

Flyhalf：フライハーフ、ス
タンドオフ《チームの司
令塔で背番号10；ハーフ
団の一員でよくボールを
蹴り上げる》
Yu Tamura：田村優
realized 〜：〜を実感した

laud 〜：〜を褒めちぎる
effort：成果

fell a win short of making
the final four：勝ってベ
スト4進出に届かなかった
involved in 〜：〜に関わった

more than I thought was
possible：期待していた
以上

quarterfinal：準々決勝
fan zone：ファンゾーン会
場《大型スクリーンでの
観戦が出来る広場》

Exercises

次の１〜５の英文を完成させるために、 a〜dの中から最も適切なものを１つ選びなさい。

1. The Japan coach of the rugby team

   a. praised the team's work ethic.

   b. complained about the players losing the game against South Africa.

   c. told the team he will not return as their coach in the future.

   d. forgot to thank the nation for their support.

2. The captain of the Brave Blossoms was

   a. Yu Tamura.

   b. Shota Horie.

   c. Michael Leitch.

   d. Jamie Joseph.

3. At the news conference, Horie

   a. expressed his optimism about the next World Cup.

   b. contrasted the reception in 2019 with the atmosphere eight years before.

   c. hoped that rugby would maintain its popularity in Japan.

   d. made all of the above comments.

4. The World Cup game this past year was held in

   a. South Africa.

   b. Japan.

   c. England.

   d. Scotland.

5. For one fan from Yokohama a highlight of the World Cup was

   a. watching the game from Oita station.

   b. dreaming of the day when Japan will win the competition.

   c. meeting and interacting with rugby-lovers from Japan and around the world.

   d. passing, and running with the ball alongside his heroes.

本文の内容に合致するものに T（True）、合致しないものに F（False）をつけなさい。

(   ) **1.** Though Japan did not win, they contributed to an historic event.

(   ) **2.** The captain of the team had few nice words to say about his coach.

(   ) **3.** One player, Yu Tamura, broke a rib in a game with South Africa.

(   ) **4.** Only 2 or 3 reporters came to the airport to see the team arrive after the 2019 tournament.

(   ) **5.** The coach is currently in serious negotiations about his contract for next year.

Vocabulary

1～12 の「rugby ground」の呼称に該当するものをイラスト a ～ l の中から 1 つ選び、（   ）内に記入しなさい。

1. crossbar (   )
2. dead ball line (   )
3. five yards line (   )
4. goal line (   )
5. goal post (   )
6. halfway line (   )
7. hooker (   )
8. referee (   )
9. scrum half (   )
10. ten yards line (   )
11. touchline (   )
12. twenty-five yards line (   )

●ロシアの科学者、安全保障上の強制捜査のショック

武装保安部隊による強制捜査を受けたモスクワにあるレベデフ物理学研究所

Photo: The New York Times ／ Redux ／アフロ

Before you read

Russian Federation
ロシア連邦
1991年12月25日ソ連崩壊により
ソビエト連邦の継承国として独立

面積　17,098,246km²（日本の約45倍）
　　　（世界1位）
首都・最大都市　モスクワ
公用語　ロシア語
人口　145,872,000人（世界9位）
民族　スラブ人　82.7%　／テュルク系　8.7%
　　　コーカサス系　3.7%　／ウラル系　1.6%
宗教　ロシア正教　63%
　　　その他のキリスト教　4.5%
　　　イスラム教　6.6%　／仏教　0.5%
　　　ユダヤ教　0.6%
識字率　99.7%
GDP　1兆6,572億米ドル（世界12位）
　　　1人当たりのGDP　11,289米ドル
　　　（世界65位）
通貨　ロシア・ルーブル
政体　共和制・連邦制

Words and Phrases

次の１〜５の語の説明として最も近いものを a〜e から１つ選び、（　）内に記入しなさい。

1. motive （　） a. educated elite
2. detonate （　） b. famous
3. illustrious （　） c. explode
4. intelligentsia （　） d. aim and reason
5. exonerate （　） e. find to have done nothing wrong

Summary

次の英文は記事の要約です。下の語群から最も適切な語を１つ選び、（　）内に記入しなさい。

2-25

　　Several Russian scientific and technological (　　　　　) have been raided by security officers. Even though (　　　　) of corruption against them are often dropped later, these events may harm their (　　　　). They also seem to (　　　　) Vladimir Putin's policy of encouraging scientists to be economic entrepreneurs. High-level political (　　　　) could be the reason for the raids.

> accusations　　contradict　　disputes　　institutions　　reputations

　　ロシアのプーチン大統領が、エリツィン元大統領の電撃辞任後の2000年３月26日に大統領に初就任してから2020年３月26日で20年となった。また、同年５月９日には、旧ソ連の対ドイツ戦勝75年を迎え、ロシア軍600機が記念飛行を披露した。プーチン大統領は、モスクワ中心部のクレムリン近くにある「無名戦士の墓」に献花し、「我々の団結があれば、無敵だと確信する」と演説、国民に結束を呼び掛けた。中国や日本、フランスなどの各国首脳臨席の下、モスクワの「赤の広場」での軍事パレードを改めて実施する方針を表明した。

　　強権的な統治でロシアに安定をもたらしたプーチン大統領は、自らの命運を左右する憲法改正案の「全国投票」を20年４月22日から延期せざるを得なくなった。「連続３選」禁止の現行憲法では、プーチン大統領は2024年の任期満了で退任だが、「全国投票」で過半数の支持を得れば、2036年まで２期12年、83歳まで大統領に君臨できる。

　　しかし、新型コロナウイルスの流行と原油価格の下落によりロシアの経済が低迷し、プーチンの影響力も危ぶまれている。軍事パレードのリハーサルが４月まで続けていたため、軍兵士が5,500人以上もコロナウイルスに感染している。20年８月８日のロシアの新型コロナウイルス感染者は87万5,378人である。

Reading

2-26

Russian security raid shocks scientists

security raid：保安部隊に
よる強制捜査

> Strikes on a physics center adds to growing
> questions about an agency's motives

The Lebedev Physics Institute in Moscow helped the
Soviet Union detonate its first nuclear bomb, figured out how
to build a hydrogen bomb and has stood for decades in the
vanguard of Russian scientific achievement. Seven of its
5 scientists have won Nobel Prizes.

Lebedev Physics Institute：
レベデフ物理学研究所
Soviet Union：ソビエト連
邦（旧ソ連）
detonate 〜：〜を爆発させる
vanguard：先導者

So it came as a shock in recent days when, shortly before
celebrations of the 85th anniversary of the illustrious institute's
founding, its halls were suddenly swarming with security
officers wearing masks and armed with automatic weapons.

came as a shock：衝撃を
与えた

swarming with 〜：〜でご
った返している

10 They searched the office of the institute's director, Nikolai
N. Kolachevsky, and questioned him for six hours about a
supposed plot to export military-use glass windows.

plot：計画

The operation set off another round of what in recent
months has become a favorite, if depressing, parlor game for
15 Russian's intelligentsia; trying to figure out why "siloviki,"
or "people of force" — security, intelligence and military
officials — have been acting so strangely and in ways at odds
with the stated policy goals of President Vladimir V. Putin.

set off another round：もう
一勝負のきっかけとなった
parlor game：室内ゲーム
siloviki：シロヴィッキ《治
安・国防関係省庁の職員
とその出身者》
people of force：公安関係者
at odds with 〜：〜と対立
する

It also provided a grim example of why, despite its
20 scientific prowess, Russia has had such trouble diversifying
its economy beyond just pulling oil, gas and other resources
out of the ground. Mr. Putin has for years called on scientists
to look beyond their books and laboratories, and use their
world-class talents to help build a modern economy.

diversifying 〜：〜を多様
化させる

called on 〜 to …：〜に
…するよう要求した

25 But those who try to do so run a serious risk of getting
raided by masked men with guns. Cases tend to drag on for
months or years, leaving the careers and nerves of suspects
shredded, even if they are eventually exonerated.

run a risk of 〜：〜する危
険を冒す
Cases：裁判事例

exonerated：無罪と認めら
れる

That happened to Dmitri Trubitsyn, a former physicist who

30 was arrested in 2017 in connection with a successful high-tech company he had set up in Siberia with fellow scientists. The case was finally closed more than a year later because of a lack of evidence to support accusations that he was running a criminal conspiracy to deceive regulators.

35 No matter what the eventual outcome of the investigation, the Lebedev Institute's Scientific Council complained in a tart statement that the recent raids had "delivered colossal reputational damage with law enforcement organs discrediting themselves in the eyes of the scientific community."

40 As with other recent examples of an increasingly aggressive and erratic security apparatus — the planting of drugs on an investigative journalist, the jailing of pacifist religious believers as "extremists" and other risibly fanciful cases — the physics institute raid has generated a swarm of
45 theories to try to explain what is going on.

One popular explanation is that the case is related to coming elections at the Russian Academy of Sciences and a bitter rivalry between the Lebedev Physics Institute and the Kurchatov Institute, a nuclear research center. Kurchatov
50 is headed by Mikhail V. Kovalchuk, whose brother, Yuri V. Kovalchuk, is a banker in St. Petersburg and an old friend and crony of Mr. Putin.

Another theory is that the F.S.B. simply needed a defense-related smuggling case to put in its annual report before the
55 end of the year.

The New York Times International Edition, November 9-10, 2019

support accusations：告発を裏付ける
criminal conspiracy：共同謀議、犯罪的陰謀

Scientific Council：科学評議会
tart statement：手厳しい声明
reputational damage：風評被害
in the eyes of ～：～の視点から見れば
As with ～：～と同様に
security apparatus：保安組織
planting of ～ on …：…に～を仕掛ける

a swarm of ～：様々な～

Kurchatov Institute：クルチャトフ研究所
brother：弟
Yuri V. Kovalchuk：ユーリ・V・コヴァルチュク《ロシアの億万長者の実業家で、「プーチンの個人銀行家」と評される金融家》
crony：取り巻き
F.S.B.：ロシア連邦保安庁《Federal Security Service(F.S.B)；ソ連時代のKGBの国内部門の後継組織》
smuggling case：密輸事件

Exercises

次の1～5の英文を完成させるために、a～dの中から最も適切なものを1つ選びなさい。

1. The Lebedev Physics Institute in Moscow is a stellar facility because
    a. it has a history of over 100 years.
    b. it campaigned against the detonation of hydrogen bombs.
    c. it built the world's first nuclear bomb.
    d. seven of their scientists have won a Nobel Prize.

2. The institute director is
    a. Vladimir V. Putin.
    b. Dmitri Trubitsyn.
    c. Nikolai N. Kolachevsky.
    d. Mikhail V. Kovalchuck.

3. A huge problem in Russia now is
    a. the strange and odd goals of Putin.
    b. security people acting against the official policies of the President.
    c. oil, gas and other resources running out.
    d. a nationwide illegal drug problem.

4. President Putin has stated that he wants
    a. scientists to come up with plans to diversify the economy.
    b. scientists to use their great skills to promote economic modernization.
    c. to steer the country away from overdependence on oil, gas and minerals.
    d. to fulfill all of the above objectives in Russia.

5. Once allegations against a scientist have been dismissed, he or she
    a. will work hard to destroy the reputation of the security services.
    b. is encouraged go join the security services.
    c. is usually able to resume their high-level work as before.
    d. may still struggle to recover their reputation.

本文の内容に合致するものに T（True）、合致しないものに F（False）をつけなさい。

(   ) **1.** Some believe the institute may have been raided because rival, Kurchatov Institute, is headed by the brother of an old friend of Mr. Putin.

(   ) **2.** The institute's physicist was found guilty of setting up a high-tech company in Siberia.

(   ) **3.** The reasons behind these raids seem to be connected more with politics than with science.

(   ) **4.** The security raids probably upset the scientists and damage their reputation.

(   ) **5.** Life in Russia appears to be the same as in other countries.

Vocabulary

次の英文は、the New York Times に掲載された *Not Just a Crisis: Coronavirus Is a Test for Putin's Security State*『単なる危機ではない：コロナウイルスはプーチンの治安状態の試金石だ』の記事の一部です。下の語群から最も適切なものを 1 つ選び、（   ）内に記入しなさい。

For Vladimir V. Putin's budding police state, the coronavirus is an (   ) dress rehearsal. As the Russian president has (   ) power, the police and security services have (   ) years upgrading their capabilities, from facial-recognition tools to crowd-control methods. Now, the spread of the virus provides a sudden test for those capabilities – and a high-stakes opportunity for Mr. Putin to win support for his hard-line measures.

Russia reported its biggest one-day jump in coronavirus cases on Thursday, with 52 new patients (   ) across 23 regions. Moscow, which has nearly half of the 199 total cases nationwide, reported the first death of a coronavirus patient in the country.

To fight the virus, Russia is taking steps to limit personal freedoms that in many ways mirror those (   ) recently by Western democracies. Schools, museums and theaters were closed nationwide, and gatherings of more than 50 people have been (   ) in Moscow and other cities. Anyone arriving from abroad is now (   ) to enter quarantine.

But for Russia, those steps carry an additional significance: they are an opportunity for Mr. Putin to show an uneasy public the effectiveness of rigid top-down governance and of a strong, (   ) state.

banned	centralized	consolidated	identified
required	spent	taken	unexpected

● ソマリアの若者たち、政府機能不全の地域に足を踏み入れる

内戦が続くソマリアの首都モガディシュで82名が死亡し、約150名が負傷した爆弾テロ現場

Photo: The New York Times ／ Redux ／ アフロ

Before you read

Federal Republic of Somalia
ソマリア連邦共和国

面積　638,000km² （日本の約1.8倍）（世界42位）
首都　モガディシュ
公用語　ソマリ語・アラビア語
人口　15,443,000人（世界73位）
民族　ソマリ族　85%
宗教　イスラム教
識字率　37.8%
GDP　4,721,000,000ドル（世界155位）
　　　1人当たりGDP　1,815ドル（世界148位）
通貨　ソマリア・シリング
政体　連邦共和制

次の１〜５の語の説明として最も近いものをa〜eから１つ選び、（　）内に記入しなさい。

1.	anemic	（　）	**a.**	lacking iron in the blood
2.	spring	（　）	**b.**	weighed down by demands
3.	overwhelmed	（　）	**c.**	torment
4.	bedevil	（　）	**d.**	increase
5.	amplify	（　）	**e.**	respond quickly and actively

Summary

次の英文は記事の要約です。下の語群から最も適切な語を１つ選び、（　）内に記入しなさい。

2-31

Somalia's government sometimes seems unable to (　　　　　) with the diseases, floods, terrorism and other problems it faces. Increasingly, however, its younger (　　　　　) are responding to crises directly. They (　　　　　) in medical facilities, organize support for (　　　　　) and even build roads. Some have returned from overseas (　　　　　) to rebuild their country.

cope	determined	generation	victims	volunteer

1886年に英国が北部を英領ソマリランドとして領有し、1908年までにイタリアが南部を領土とした。1960年7月1日英領北部とイタリア領南部が統合、独立し、ソマリア共和国が発足した。1969年のクーデターによりバレ政権が実権を握り、ソマリ社会主義革命党の一党独裁体制となった。1988年に内戦勃発、91年にバレ政権が崩壊した。

崩壊以来2007年まで、ソマリアは全土を実効的に支配する中央政府が存在しない状態が続いた。劣悪な治安の下、大量の難民及び国内避難民が発生し、また干ばつの深刻化等により、食糧不足が悪化する等、重大な人道危機が生じた。

2012年9月にハッサン・モハムドが大統領に選出され、21年振りに統一政府が樹立された。2017年には、モハメド・ファルマージョが新大統領に選出された。アラブ・アフリカ諸国との友好関係の維持を外交の基盤とし、国造りと国際社会の支援を要請している。

ソマリア沖・アデン湾の海賊発生件数は、近年低い水準で推移している。一方、海賊を生み出す根本原因の1つであるソマリア国内の貧困や若者の就職難等は未だ解決しておらず、海賊による脅威は引き続き存在している。経済も壊滅状態で、最貧国の1つである。

Reading

2-32

Young Somalis Step in Where Government Fails

MOGADISHU, Somalia — She had just finished battling the floods, and then the bomb went off.

For a month of 10-hour days, Dr. Amina Abdulkadir Isack, 27, tended to anemic mothers, children with malaria
5 and pregnant women as a volunteer in central Somalia, where record floods had left thousands of people in dire need of help the government could scarcely provide.

2-33

But only days after she came home, on a hot Mogadishu morning in late December, terrorists detonated an explosives-
10 laden truck in a busy intersection, killing 82 people and injuring nearly 150, including university students studying to become health specialists and doctors like her.

Dr. Isack sprang right back into action, helping a youth-led crisis response team of volunteers who tracked the victims,
15 called their families, collected donations and performed many services the government was too overwhelmed to manage on its own.

"The youth are the ones who build nations," Dr. Isack said. "We have to rely on ourselves."

2-34
20 Much like the floods before it, the attack in Mogadishu, the deadliest in Somalia in more than two years, underscored the feeble emergency response in a nation that is no stranger to natural and man-made disasters. The Somali government struggles to provide basic public services like health care and
25 education, let alone a comprehensive response to emergencies.

Yet in the face of the country's mounting challenges — from a changing climate to the indiscriminate violence of terrorism — young Somalis are increasingly getting organized and bootstrapping their way out of crises, rather than waiting
30 on help from their government or its foreign backers.

2-35 Government officials say they do respond to the country's emergencies, including establishing a national committee

---

went off：爆発した

For a month of 10-hour days：1日10時間を一か月間

tended to ～：～の世話をした

anemic：貧血症の

busy intersection：人通りの多い交差点

sprang back into action：勢いよく仕事を再開した

crisis response team of ～：～から成る危機対応チーム

tacked ～：～の身元を確認した

donations：寄付

on its own：自力では

underscored ～：～を明確に示した

no stranger to ～：～を全く知らないわけではない

let alone ～：～は言うまでもなく

indiscriminate：無差別な

organized：組織化された

bootstrapping their way out of ～：自力で～からの脱出を試みる

---

to aid the victims of the Dec. 28 attack. Turkey and Qatar airlifted dozens of the badly injured. But many youth activists in Somalia say that the response from the authorities is often tardy or inadequate, making it all the more essential for citizens like themselves to jump in and help fill the gaps.

Somalia has experienced one degree or another of chaos for almost three decades, bedeviled first by clan infighting and then by violent extremism. But through it all, Somalis have found ways to not only establish thriving businesses, but also take on core state services like building roads and providing health care and education.

This independent spirit was amplified after militants with the Shabab, a terrorist group affiliated with Al Qaeda, surrendered control of Mogadishu in 2011, effectively leaving the capital in the hands of an internationally-backed but weak government that has often been unable to secure the capital, much less the country.

Since then, young Somalis, including members of the diaspora who have returned home, have taken a leading role in the stabilization and rebuilding process. They have worked on rehabilitating child soldiers, reviving domestic tourism, responding to humanitarian crises, organizing book fairs and even selling Somali camels to customers using bitcoin.

The New York Times, February 16, 2020

---

tardy or inadequate：遅いか不充分な

all the more：増々

one degree or another of ～：程度の差がある～

bedeviled：苦しめられる
clan infighting：クラン（氏族・部族）間の内紛

take on ～：～に取り組む

core state services：国家による中核となるサービス

Shabab：アル・シャバブ《ソマリア南部を中心に活動するイスラム勢力》

Al Qaeda：アル・カイダ、国際イスラム戦線《アラビア語で「墓地」の意；国際的なテロのネットワーク》

surrendered control of ～：～の支配権を放棄した

leaving ～ in the hands of …：～を…の手に委ねる

much less ～：まして～ではない

diaspora who have returned home：国から離散したが帰国した人たち

stabilization：安定化

worked on ～：～に取り組んできた

rehabilitating ～：～の更生

bitcoin：ビットコイン《インターネット上の仮想通貨の一種》

Exercises

Multiple Choice

次の１～２の英文の質問に答え、３～５の英文を完成させるために、ａ～ｄの中から最も適切なものを１つ選びなさい。

1. Which group is credited in this article with keeping Somalia moving?

   a. Young Somalians.
   b. The government officials.
   c. The militants with Shabab.
   d. Turkish and Qatari aid-givers.

2. How many people were killed or injured in the bomb attack?

   a. 82 killed and 150 injured
   b. 150 killed and 82 injured.
   c. 230 killed and 15 injured.
   d. 380 killed.

3. The government has argued that it

   a. was tardy in dealing with natural disasters.
   b. depends entirely on youthful volunteers.
   c. cannot build roads without receiving foreign aid.
   d. responded to the bomb attack.

4. At only 27, Dr. Isack found herself having to

   a. surrender control of Mogadishu.
   b. defuse explosives loaded onto a truck in a busy intersection.
   c. enter politics because of the lack of government leadership.
   d. handle a major flood and organize volunteers to help bomb victims.

5. Somalia has had the kind of problems mentioned in this article for

   a. three years.
   b. thirteen decades.
   c. thirty years.
   d. a third of its history.

本文の内容に合致するものにT（True）、合致しないものにF（False）をつけなさい。

(   ) **1.** The government's response to emergencies is generally adequate.

(   ) **2.** Somalia has done better since Al Qaeda surrendered control over Mogadishu, allowing the spirit of young Somalians to shine.

(   ) **3.** Two of the challenges of Somalia are a changing climate and terrorist attacks.

(   ) **4.** It is not difficult for the country to acquire capital.

(   ) **5.** Malaria still exists in Mogadishu.

Vocabulary

次の１〜８は、アフリカ中・東部の国々に関する英文です。 下記の国名から１つ選び（   ）内に、a〜hを地図から選び、[   ]内に記入しなさい。

1. (   ) has borders with Djibouti, Ethiopia, and Kenya and its capital is Mogadishu.   [   ]

2. (   ) is a country in eastern Africa and its capital is Addis Ababa.   [   ]

3. (   )'s capital is Nairobi and its main languages are English and Swahili.   [   ]

4. (   ) is a small country and has a border with Somalia and Ethiopia.   [   ]

5. (   ) is a united republic in the east with an Indian Ocean coast.   [   ]

6. (   )'s people are called Rwandan.   [   ]

7. (   ) is a country in the eastern central region and its capital is Kampala.   [   ]

8. (   ) has borders with Congo, Rwanda, and Tanzania.   [   ]

Burundi	Djibouti
Ethiopia	Kenya
Rwanda	Somalia
Tanzania	Uganda

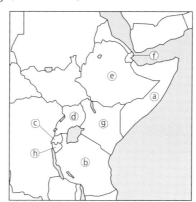

● 新国籍法への反対運動が荒れ狂うが、インドは ヒンドゥ教国となるのか

インドでイスラム教徒を除外する新国籍法を巡り、抗議するデモ参加者たち

Photo: ロイター／アフロ

Before you read

Republic of India　インド

面積　3,287,590km²（日本の8.7倍）（世界 7 位）
人口　1,310,000,000人（世界 2 位）
首都　ニューデリー　／ デリー連邦直轄地
最大都市　ムンバイ
公用語　英語、ヒンドゥ語
民族　インド・アーリア族　72%
　　　ドラヴィダ族　25%
　　　モンゴロイド族　3 %
宗教　ヒンドゥ教　79.8%
　　　イスラム教　14.2%
　　　キリスト教　2.3%　／ シーク教　1.7%
　　　仏教　0.7%　／ ジャイナ教　0.4%
GDP　2 兆7,187億ドル（世界 7 位）
　　　　1 人当たり GDP　2,038ドル（世界144位）
通貨　インド・ルピー
識字率　75.6%
政体　共和制

次の1〜5の語句の説明として最も近いものをa〜eから1つ選び、(　)内に記入しなさい。

1. round up　　　(　　)　　**a.** centered on religion

2. overt　　　　(　　)　　**b.** cut or disconnect

3. shut down　　(　　)　　**c.** open and obvious

4. wrench　　　(　　)　　**d.** arrest many people

5. theocratic　　(　　)　　**e.** pull forcefully

Summary

次の英文は記事の要約です。下の語群から最も適切な語を1つ選び、(　)内に記入しなさい。

2-37

The Modi government says its new citizenship law will (　　　　) immigrants. However, the measure (　　　　) Muslims. The government argues that it is (　　　　) who need support as they are often escaping Muslim-majority countries. But India's large Muslim (　　　　) claims this is part of a campaign to (　　　　) against them and strengthen the Hindu majority.

discriminate　　excludes　　help　　minority　　non-Muslims

2019年12月に、インドの議会で改正国籍法が可決され、成立した。従来の国籍法に、イスラム教徒ではないバングラディシュとパキスタンとアフガニスタンから2014年末までにインドに逃れてきた不法移民に対して国籍を与えるとする条項が加わった。イスラム教徒は対象外で、ヒンドゥ教、仏教、キリスト教、ジャイナ教などの6宗教の信者で、迫害を受けた宗教的少数者を想定している。

3か国であるバングラディシュには88.4%、パキスタンは97%、アフガニスタン99%のイスラム教徒がいて、大多数を占めている。しかし、この改正国籍法では、イスラム教徒は対象外になり、最終的にイスラム教徒だけが不法滞在者となってしまう。これは、イスラム教の排除につながり、宗教対立が起きている。首都ニューデリーでは、52名の死者が出て、惨事となった。この改正国籍法への賛成派と反対派による大規模な衝突も起きているが、モディ首相は強気の姿勢を崩していない。

モディ首相率いる与党インド人民党は、ヒンドゥ教に基づく国家運営を目指すヒンドゥ教至上主義を掲げている。しかし、インドもコロナウイルス感染拡大防止のため、2020年4月から Lockdown が続いている。

Reading

2-38

As Protests Rage on Citizenship Bill, Is India Becoming a Hindu Nation?

NEW DELHI — Prime Minister Narendra Modi's government has rounded up thousands of Muslims in Kashmir, revoked the area's autonomy and enforced a citizenship test in northeastern India that left nearly two million people
5 potentially stateless, many of them Muslim.

But it was Mr. Modi's gamble to pass a sweeping new citizenship law that favors every South Asian faith other than Islam that has set off days of widespread protests.

2-39

The law, which easily passed both houses of Parliament
10 last week, is the most overt sign, opponents say, that Mr. Modi intends to turn India into a Hindu-centric state that would leave the country's 200 million Muslims at a calculated disadvantage.

Indian Muslims, who have watched anxiously as Mr.
15 Modi's government has pursued a Hindu nationalist program, have finally erupted in anger. Over the past few days, protests have broken in cities across the country.

Mr. Modi's government has responded by calling out troops, shutting down the internet and imposing curfews, just
20 as it did when it clamped down on Kashmir. In New Delhi, police officers beat unarmed students with wooden poles, dragging them away and sending scores to the hospital. In Assam, they shot and killed several young men.

2-40

India's Muslims had stayed relatively quiet during the
25 other recent setbacks, keenly aware of the electoral logic that has pushed them to the margins. India is about 80 percent Hindu, and 14 percent Muslim, and Mr. Modi and his party won a crushing election victory in May and handily control the Parliament.

30 But Indian Muslims are feeling increasingly desperate, and so are progressives, many Indians of other faiths, and

Citizenship Bill：国籍法《改正法でインドに住む不法移民にインド国籍を与えるのが目的》

rounded up ～：～を逮捕した

revoked ～：～を取り消した、無効にした

autonomy：自治権

favors ～：～をえこひいきする

other than ～：～以外の

both houses：上下両院

opponents：反対派

calculated disadvantage：事前に目論まれた不利益

nationalist：民族主義的

erupted in anger：怒りを爆発させた

broken：突然発生した

curfews：（夜間）外出禁止令

clamped down on ～：～を弾圧した

setbacks：敗北、後退

keenly aware of ～：～を痛感させられる

his party：インド人民党

progressives：進歩主義者

those who see a secular government as fundamental to India's identity and its future.

The world is now weighing in, too. United Nations officials, American representatives, international advocacy groups and religious organizations have issued scathing statements saying that the citizenship law is blatantly discriminatory. Some are even calling for sanctions.

Critics are deeply worried that Mr. Modi is trying to wrench India away from its secular, democratic roots and turn this nation of 1.3 billion people into a religious state, a homeland for Hindus.

"They want a theocratic state," said B.N. Srikrishna, a former judge on India's Supreme Court. "This is pushing the country to the brink, to the brink of chaos."

Mr. Modi is no stranger to communal violence. The worst bloodshed that India has seen in recent years exploded on his watch, in 2002, in Gujarat, when he was the top official in the state and clashes between Hindus and Muslims killed more than 1,000 people — most of them Muslims.

The new citizenship legislation, called the Citizenship Amendment Act, expedites Indian citizenship for migrants from some of India's neighboring countries if they are Hindu, Christian, Buddhist, Sikh, Parsee or Jain. Only one major religion in South Asia was left off: Islam.

Indian officials have denied any anti-Muslim bias and said the measure was intended purely to help persecuted minorities migrating from India's predominantly Muslim neighbors — Pakistan, Afghanistan and Bangladesh.

The New York Times, December 16, 2019

---

secular government：非宗教政権

weighing in：介入する

representatives：国会議員

advocacy groups：権利擁護団体

discriminatory：差別的な

sanctions：制裁

Critics：批判する人たち

homeland：国土

theocratic state：神政国家

Supreme Court：最高裁判所

communal violence：対立住民間の暴力

on his watch：彼の当番の時に

top official：知事

Citizenship Amendment Act：改正国籍法

Sikh：シーク教徒《パンジャーブ地方の宗教；合理的、現実的、寛容な教えが特徴》

Parsee：パーシー教徒《インドに住むゾロアスター教徒（拝火教教徒）》

Jain：ジャイナ教徒《「不害」の禁戒を厳守するなど徹底した苦行・禁欲主義が特徴》

left off：除外された

persecuted：迫害されている

Exercises

Multiple Choice

次の1〜5の英文を完成させるために、a〜dの中から最も適切なものを1つ選びなさい。

1. Kashmir's Muslims are incensed because

    a. Prime Minister Modi rounded up thousands of Muslims and revoked Kashmir's autonomy.

    b. two million illegal migrants in northeastern India were given citizenship.

    c. of recent comments about India by United Nations.

    d. of all of the above events.

2. India's Muslims are complaining of

    a. the government pursuing a Hindu national program.

    b. the increasingly secular character of the Modi government.

    c. discrimination by international organizations and religious groups.

    d. all of the above developments.

3. Currently India's population is

    a. 14% Muslim and 80% Hindu.

    b. 14% Hindu and 80% Muslim.

    c. 40% Hindu and 60% Muslim.

    d. 60% Hindu and 40% Muslim.

4. The new citizenship legislation that Prime Minister Modi wanted will expedite citizenship for migrants

    a. practicing Hinduism or Christianity.

    b. belonging to the Shia sect.

    c. from Kashmir's Muslim community.

    d. fleeing persecution by Christians.

5. Supporters of Prime Minster Modi's policies include

    a. United Nations officials.

    b. American representatives.

    c. radical Hindus nationalists.

    d. all of the above political and religious interests.

本文の内容に合致するものに T（True）、合致しないものに F（False）をつけなさい。

(   )   **1.**   Prime Minister Modi has previously never used violence during his rule.

(   )   **2.**   Protests within the Muslim community have broken out to complain about the anti-Muslim policies.

(   )   **3.**   Progressives in India want a secular government for India and its future.

(   )   **4.**   The new citizenship bill may not pass in Parliament.

(   )   **5.**   When Mr. Modi was the top official in Gujarat in 2002, fighting between Muslims and Hindus cost 1,000 people their lives.

Vocabulary

次の１～８は、イスラム教とヒンドゥ教、仏教に関する語です。下の a ～ h の説明文の中から最も適切なものを１つ選び、（　　）内に記入しなさい。

1.   burka   (　　　　)
2.   Hinduism   (　　　　)
3.   Islam   (　　　　)
4.   Koran   (　　　　)
5.   nirvana   (　　　　)
6.   Ramadan   (　　　　)
7.   reincarnation   (　　　　)
8.   Siva   (　　　　)

a.   a state of knowledge reached while meditating

b.   the ninth month of the Muslim year, during which no food or drink may be taken between sunrise and sunset

c.   the predominant religion of the Indian subcontinent

d.   the holy book of the Muslims

e.   a long enveloping garment worn in public by Muslim women

f.   the destroyer; one of the three Hindu major divinities

g.   returning to life in a new body after death

h.   the Muslim religion, and the people and countries that practice this religion

●急激な変化：ガイアナは石油で裕福になったが、 民族間の緊張も増大

農業国から産油国へと急激に変化しつつあるガイアナの首都ジョージタウンの護岸沿いに建設中のビル群　　　Photo: The New York Times ／ Redux ／アフロ

Before you read

Republic of Guyana
ガイアナ共和国
1966年英国より独立

面積　215,000km²（本州よりやや小さい）（世界83位）
人口　783,000人（世界164位）
公用語　英語、ガイアナ・クレオール語
首都　ジョージタウン
民族　東インド系　30.8%
　　　アフリカ系　29.3%
　　　混血　19.9%
　　　先住民族　10.5%　／その他　0.5%
宗教　キリスト教カトリック　8.1%
　　　　　　プロテスタント　16.9%
　　　　　　イギリス国教会　6.9%
　　　ヒンドゥ教　28.4%
　　　イスラム教　7.2%
GDI　38億9900万米ドル（世界159位）
　　　1人当たり GDI　4,984米ドル（世界104位）
通貨　ガイアナ・ドル
政体　立憲共和制
識字率　85.6%

次の 1〜5 の語の説明として最も近いものを a〜e から 1 つ選び、（　　）内に記入しなさい。

1. sprawling 　　（　　）　　a. low-lying and extensive
2. shrub 　　　　（　　）　　b. poorly-built house
3. shack 　　　　（　　）　　c. causing great harm to
4. devastating 　（　　）　　d. bush or small tree
5. paralysis 　　（　　）　　e. inability to act

Summary

次の英文は記事の要約です。下の語群から最も適切な語を 1 つ選び、（　　）内に記入しなさい。

🎧
2-43

Guyana hopes to transform its poor, (　　　　　　) economy by exploiting its oil resources. While many citizens see prospects for new (　　　　　), those making a living from sugar cane production are unhappy, with thousands of them now (　　　　　). Despite government promises to (　　　　　) sugar workers, the opposition says rural (　　　　　) are dying.

agricultural 　　 communities 　　 retrain 　　 unemployed 　　 wealth

ガイアナ共和国は、1966年5月に英連邦の1国として独立した。南アメリカ大陸で唯一英語が公用語の国である。1498年コロンブスが渡来、翌99年にヴェスプッチが上陸した。イギリス人の入植が行われたが、1621年以降は、オランダ西インド会社の管轄下に入り、18世紀までオランダの植民地となった。1814年からイギリスの植民地となり、British Guiana となった。奴隷制度廃止後、インド系移民が34万人近く流入し、サトウキビ農園労働者となった。

独立後、黒人勢力を代表する人民国民会議 PNC とインド系で社会主義の人民進歩党 PPP との間で人種的対立が起こり、政情不安が続いている。総選挙の度に暴動が起き、2020年3月の選挙でも両党の中傷が止まず、支持層への偏った利益誘導や人種対立で分断に拍車がかかった。

米石油エクソンモービルが、2015年に首都ジョージタウンの200km 沖合に海底油田を発見し、19年12月に原油生産を開始した。推定埋蔵量は80億バレルに上ると言われている。IMF は、2020年の経済成長率が前年の4.4％から85.6％に急上昇すると予測している。しかし、新型コロナウイルスの流行で移動制限や経済活動の停滞、原油価格の低下が影を落としている。さらに人種対立も収まっていない。

Reading

2-44

'It Changed So Fast':
Oil Is Making Guyana Wealthy
but Intensifying Tensions

Intensifying 〜：〜を強める

GEORGETOWN, Guyana — On a sprawling abandoned sugar estate by the coast of Guyana, the scale of the changes sweeping across the country is immediately visible.

sugar estate：砂糖農園

In just a few years, enormous warehouses and office buildings servicing international oil companies have sprung up amid the shrub land, irrigation canals and fields of wild cane.

wild cane：野生のサトウキビ

2-45

People are "moving from cutting cane to businessmen," said Mona Harisha, a local shop owner. "It changed so fast."

Guyana is giving up its past as an agricultural economy and speeding toward its near-term future as an oil-producing giant. And so Ms. Harisha has renovated her general goods shop, redolent of Indian spices, which she runs from a side of her cottage in the Houston neighborhood of Georgetown, the county's capital.

agricultural economy：農業経済国

giant：強国

from a side of 〜：〜の一角で

Houston neighborhood：ヒューストン地区

For many, the transformation into an oil economy has brought optimism about greater prosperity. But that optimism is often mixed with a fatalism that nothing will really improve for the vast majority of people in one of South America's poorest countries.

optimism：楽観主義

fatalism：運命論

2-46

In a brick shack on the edge of the jungle 15 miles away from Houston, Jason Bobb-Semple, 25, is making his own big bet on oil.

making a big bet on 〜：〜に大きな賭けをする

With a $3,000 government loan, he built a small poultry farm and bought 4,000 chicks to meet what he expects to be a booming food demand in a rapidly developing country.

poultry farm：養鶏場

meet 〜：〜を満たす、〜に対応する

food demand：食糧需要

Just hours after Mr. Bobb-Semple received the chicks, he got a visit from his first potential investor, a Guyanese émigré businessman who was back home looking for eggs to sell to the offshore oil rigs.

potential investor：投資者になりそうな人

Guyanese émigré：ガイアナから外国に移住（亡命）した人

The investor, Lancelot Myers, said oil companies currently have to import most of their provisions, providing a business opportunity to local entrepreneurs who can fill supply gaps. "Now is the time to hit the ground running," he said.

35　The enterprising energy of the Guyanese seeking to benefit from the oil boom contrasts sharply with the deep depression, both economic and psychological, reining in the rural sugar belt, which had powered this country's economy since the 17th century.

40　A decision by the current president, David A. Granger, to shut down most of Guyana's unprofitable, state-owned cane processing plants in 2018 left about 7,000 sugar workers unemployed, devastating the surrounding regions.

The closures have turned places like Skeldon in the fertile
45　east of the country into ghost towns, wiping out the once vibrant local markets and businesses that used to serve the sugar workers.

The layoffs inflamed ethnic tensions, with the mainly Indo-Guyanese sugar workers accusing the predominantly black
50　government of Mr. Granger of targeted economic repression.

The ruling party advocates using the money to retrain agricultural workers for the public and service sectors. The opposition instead wants to subsidize sugar farms to keep rural communities alive.

55　The International Monetary Fund projected that Guyana's tiny economy would grow by 86 percent this year, the fastest rate in the world. That forecast, however, is likely to take a major hit from the sudden collapse of oil prices, the coronavirus pandemic and Guyana's ongoing political paralysis.

The New York Times, April 7, 2020

provisions：食糧

supply gaps：供給ギャップ

hit the ground running：新しいことに直ぐに全力で取り組む

reining in ～：～を抑える、弱める

cane processing plants：サトウキビ加工工場

used to ～：かつては～していた

layoffs：一時解雇

ethnic tensions：民族間の緊張

Indo-Guyanese：インド系ガイアナ人《1834年に奴隷制度が廃止されると、砂糖工場の労働者としてインド人が導入された》

accusing ～ of …：～を…だと非難する

targeted economic repression：自分たちを標的にした経済的抑圧

ruling party：与党

the money：石油収入

public sector：公共部門

subsidize ～：～に助成金を払う

International Monetary Fund：国際通貨基金 (IMF)《国際金融や為替相場の安定化を目的として設立された国際連合の専門機関》

fastest rate：最大の伸び率

take a major hit from ～：～によって大損害を被る

collapse：暴落

ongoing：現在進行中の

paralysis：マヒ状態

Exercises

次の１～２の英文の質問に答え、３～５の英文を完成させるために、ａ～ｄの中から最も適切なものを１つ選びなさい。

1. What has changed in Guyana?

     a. Poultry farms are all over the city.

     b. Sugar canes estates are now flourishing.

     c. There is a new oil economy.

     d. The economy has grown by 86%.

2. What occurred when David Granger shut down sugar cane estates?

     a. Citizens started purchasing more chickens.

     b. 7,000 workers lost their jobs.

     c. The government supplied new jobs for displaced workers.

     d. The employment patterns of agricultural workers went unchanged.

3. Guyana is changing into an oil economy, which means

     a. there is a chance of greater prosperity.

     b. many citizens are expecting a more comfortable life.

     c. some citizens are likely to get left behind.

     d. all of the above developments are expected.

4. Mr. Bobb-Semple's chicken investment

     a. has failed because people can no longer afford to buy eggs.

     b. seems to be paying off now that he is to supply eggs to the oil rigs.

     c. has badly affected the economy of towns like Skeldon.

     d. seems likely to end in financial disaster.

5. Guyana has been involved in the process of sugar cane since

     a. the 16th century.

     b. the 17th century.

     c. the 18th century.

     d. the 19th century.

本文の内容に合致するものにＴ（True）、合致しないものにＦ（False）をつけなさい。

(   ) **1.** Guyana's ruling party says it will retrain agricultural workers for public sector and service employment.

(   ) **2.** The opposition wants to subsidize sugar to keep rural towns alive.

(   ) **3.** Local markets and business in most rural towns continue to thrive.

(   ) **4.** The International Monetary Fund predictions for Guyana's growth look to be fairly accurate.

(   ) **5.** There is currently a recession in parts of Guyana caused by the changes in their economy.

Vocabulary

次の１～８の英文は、貧富に関することわざです。日本文に合わせて、下の語群の中から最も適切な語を１つ選び、（   ）内に記入しなさい。

1. 金がものを言う世の中だ。
Money is (   ) in this world of ours.

2. 貧乏くじを引いてしまった。
He drew the short (   ).

3. 金に糸目をつけない。
He is (   ) with his money.

4. 金持ち苦労多し。
Much coin, much (   ).

5. 金の切れ目が縁の切れ目。
When poverty comes in, love (   ) out of the windows.

6. 金持ちの食道楽、貧乏人の子沢山。
Rich men feed, poor men (   ).

7. 金持ち喧嘩せず。
A rich man never (   ).

8. 貧乏暇なし。
Poor men have no (   ).

breed	care	everything	flies
free	leisure	quarrels	straw

Unit **22**

● ハイチ、崖っぷちに追い込まれる

政治紛争による暴力と沈滞のせいで崩壊寸前のハイチでの反政府デモ

Photo: The New York Times ／ Redux ／アフロ

Before you read

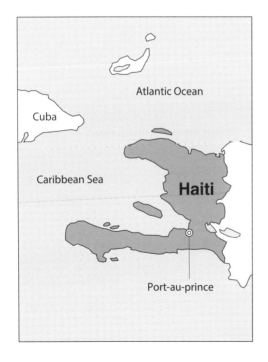

Republic of Haiti
ハイチ共和国
1804年フランスより独立

面積	27,750km²（北海道の約３分の１）（世界143位）
人口	11,263,000人（世界83位）
首都	ポルトーフランス
公用語	フランス語、ハイチ・クレオール語
識字率	52.9%
民族	アフリカ系　95%　その他　5％
宗教	キリスト教カトリック　95%　ブードゥ教
GDP	89億1,500万米ドル（世界142位）１人当たりGDP　800米ドル（世界171位）
通貨	グールド
政体	立憲共和制

次の１〜５の語句の説明として最も近いものをa〜eから１つ選び、（　　）内に記入しなさい。

1. stagnation （　　）   a. sickness or weakness
2. cling to （　　）   b. bitter feeling
3. malaise （　　）   c. hold desperately
4. ouster （　　）   d. lack of development of progress
5. acrimony （　　）   e. removal

Summary

　次の英文は記事の要約です。下の語群から最も適切な語を１つ選び、（　　）内に記入しなさい。

2-49

　The poorest country in the (　　　　　　) is used to economic and political crises. But things have become even worse in Haiti because of a power (　　　　　　) between the US-supported president and the opposition. Business, schools and transport have stopped (　　　　　　). Underresourced hospitals sometimes have to make (　　　　　) decisions about who to (　　　　　).

| Americas | functioning | heartbreaking | struggle | treat |

　ハイチは、イスパニョーラ島西部に位置し、東にドミニカ共和国と国境を接し、カリブ海の北西にキューバ、西にジャマイカが存在する。1804年に南北アメリカ大陸でアメリカ合衆国に次ぎ、２番目に独立した黒人による共和制国家である。1492年にコロンブスがイスパニョーラ島を発見し、スペイン人にネイティブのアラワク人が絶滅させられた。その後、西アフリカの黒人奴隷らが運ばれて来た。1697年に島の西側３分の１つまり現在のハイチをフランス領とし、黒人奴隷を酷使し、林業、サトウキビ、コーヒーの栽培で巨万の富を築いた。

　しかし、独立以来現在に至るまで国家分裂・反乱、さらに地震やハリケーン、コレラ等の大規模な災害が相次ぎ、大混乱に拍車がかけられている。ハイチの１人当たりのGDPは870ドルで、アメリカ大陸の35か国中最貧国である。国民の80％が劣悪な貧困状態に置かれている。人口の３分の２が農業に従事しているが、農業インフラの不十分、過耕作、土地の荒廃で農業生産性は極めて低い。人口の約半数が慢性的栄養失調状態である。ハイチ人の95％がアフリカ系で、黒人と白人の混血ムラートとの間には、経済的・文化的・社会的に格差が大きい。カトリック信者が95％を占めているが、ベナンにルーツのあるブードゥ教の慣習も行っている。

Reading

A nation pushed to the brink

Political struggle brings violence and stagnation to impoverished Haiti

The small hospital was down to a single day's supply of oxygen and had to decide who would get it: the adults recovering from strokes and other ailments, or the newborns clinging to life in the neonatal ward.

5   Haiti's political crisis had forced this awful dilemma — one drama of countless in a nation driven to the brink of collapse.

A struggle between President Jovenel Moïse and a surging opposition movement demanding his ouster has led
10 to violent demonstrations and barricaded streets across the country, rendering roads impassable and creating a sprawling emergency.

Caught in the national paralysis, officials at Sainte Croix Hospital were forced to choose who might live and who might
15 die.

Fortunately, a truck carrying 40 fresh tanks of oxygen made it through at the last minute, giving the hospital a reprieve.

Though the country has been trapped for years in cycles
20 of political and economic dysfunction, many Haitians say the current crisis is worse than anything they have experienced. Lives that were already extremely difficult, here in the poorest country in the Western Hemisphere, have become even more so.

25   Weeks of unrest around Haiti, coupled with rampant corruption and economic malaise, have led to soaring prices, a disintegration of public services and a galloping sense of insecurity and lawlessness. At least 30 people have been killed in the demonstrations in the past few weeks, 15 of them
30 by police officers, according to the United Nations.

brink：（崖などの）縁（ふち）

Political struggle：政治紛争（闘争）

stagnation：沈滞

impoverished：貧しい、貧困に陥った

down to 〜：〜まで不足する、下がる

strokes：脳卒中

neonatal ward：新生児病棟

ouster：追放、罷免

Caught in 〜：〜に巻き込まれて

made it through：上手く切り抜けた

reprieve：一時的救済

dysfunction：機能不全

Western Hemisphere：西半球

unrest：不安

rampant corruption：蔓延する汚職

malaise：低迷

soaring prices：高騰する物価

2-53

Gas shortages are worsening by the day. Hospitals have cut services or closed entirely. Public transportation has ground to a halt. Businesses have shuttered. Most schools have been closed since early September, leaving millions of children idle. Widespread layoffs have compounded chronic poverty and hunger. Uncertainty hangs over everything.

Many Haitians with the means to flee have left or are planning to, while most who remain are simply trying to figure out where they are going to get their next meals.

Haiti was once a strategic ally for the United States, which often played a crucial role here. During the Cold War, American governments supported — albeit at times grudgingly — the authoritarian governments of François Duvalier and his son, Jean-Claude Duvalier, because of their anti-Communist stance.

2-54

In 1994, the Clinton administration sent troops to restore Jean-Bertrand Aristide to power after his ouster as president, but 10 years later, intense pressure from the United States helped push Mr. Aristide out again.

Now, protestors are criticizing the United States for continuing to stand by Mr. Moïse. The Trump administration has urged respect for the democratic process, but has said little about the unrest in Haiti.

The current crisis is a culmination of more than a year of violent protests, and the product, in part, of political acrimony that has seized the nation since Mr. Moïse, a businessman, took office in February 2017 following an electoral process that was marred by delays, allegations of voter fraud and an abysmal voter turnout.

The New York Times International Edition, October 23, 2019

Gas：ガソリン
by the day：日に日に

ground to a halt：急停止した

compounded 〜：〜を悪化させた
poverty and hunger：貧困と飢餓

figure out 〜：（答えを）見つけ出す
strategic ally：戦略的同盟国
Cold War：（東西）（米ソ）冷戦《第二次大戦後、世界を二分した資本主義・自由主義国陣営と共産主義・社会主義国陣営との対立構造》
albeit 〜：〜ではあるが
authoritarian governments：独裁政権
restore 〜 to power as president：〜を大統領として権力の座に復帰させる

criticizing 〜 for …：〜を…だと非難する
stand by 〜：〜を支持する
urged 〜：〜を要請した

culmination：頂点
product：産物《culmination と同じく補語》
acrimony：峻烈性、厳しさ
took office：就任した
marred：損なわれた
delays：（選挙実施の）先延ばし
allegations of voter fraud：不正投票の申し立て
abysmal voter turnout：ひどい投票率

Exercises

Multiple Choice

次の１〜５の英文を完成させるために、ａ〜ｄの中から最も適切なものを１つ選びなさい。

1. The recent problems at Sainte Croix Hospital

    a. caused political discord.

    b. were the result of bad weather.

    c. happened because they refused to treat sick people.

    d. were solved, temporarily, just in time.

2. According to this article, Haiti's current political unrest

    a. was caused mainly by the Clinton administration.

    b. has worsened because of statements by the Trump administration.

    c. happened because citizens returned to the country for a better life.

    d. has triggered one of its worse economic crises.

3. One reason given for Haitian hospitals' lack of supplies is that

    a. transport routes are being blocked during this unrest.

    b. oxygen tanks have been stolen by the army.

    c. many health workers support communist groups.

    d. shipments of food from other countries have been blocked by the U.S.

4. The article suggests that corrupt practices surrounded the election of

    a. Duvalier the elder.

    b. Duvalier the younger.

    c. Jovenel Moïse.

    d. Jean-Bertrand Aristide.

5. The word "abysmal" tells us that

    a. a high number of citizens voted.

    b. a low number of citizens voted.

    c. voters were subject to violence.

    d. voters made a very unwise choice.

本文の内容に合致するものに T (True)、合致しないものに F (False) をつけなさい。

(   ) **1.** The hospital ended up letting patients die because of lack of oxygen.

(   ) **2.** The current President of Haiti is Jovenel Moïse.

(   ) **3.** Jean-Bertrand Aristide was President of Haiti only one time.

(   ) **4.** Fortunately no one has been killed in all of the demonstrations that are paralyzing Haitians' life.

(   ) **5.** The current President of the United States has vowed to intervene in the unrest in Haiti.

Vocabulary

次のクロスワードパズルを、下の Across 横、Down 縦の英文説明を読んで、Unit 22 の記事から最も適切な語句を見つけ、□の中に 1 文字ずつ入れなさい。

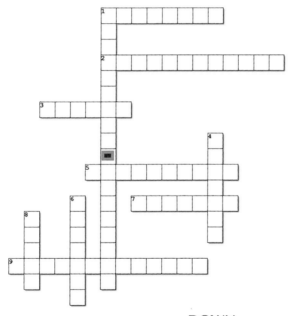

ACROSS
1. the name of two Haitian presidents
2. very poor
3. one of Haiti's main languages
5. reluctantly
7. personal name of current president
9. like a dictator

DOWN
1. Haiti's eastern neighbor
4. ailment
6. baby
8. cheating

Unit 23

● 独立20年後、経済的困窮の東ティモールに中国が援助の手を

有望な天然ガス田があるが経済的困窮に苦しむ東ティモールの首都ディリ市内のマーケット

Photo: Alamy ／アフロ

Before you read

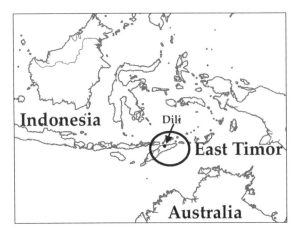

Democratic Republic of Timor-Leste
東ティモール民主共和国

面積　14,900km²（東京・千葉・埼玉・神奈川の合
　　　計面積とほぼ同じ）（世界154位）
首都　ディリ
公用語　テトゥン語、ポルトガル語（インドネシア
　　　　語・英語も使用）
人口　1,293,000人（世界156位）／ 識字率　50.1%
民族　メラネシア系が大多数、マレー系、中国系
宗教　キリスト教カトリック　99.1%
　　　イスラム教　0.79%
GDP　2,746,000,000米ドル（世界165位）
　　　１人当たり GDP　2,164米ドル（世界143位）
通貨　米ドル ／ 政体　共和制

Words and Phrases

次の 1 ～ 5 の語の説明として最も近いものを a ～ e から 1 つ選び、(　　)内に記入しなさい。

1. crow　　　　　　(　　)　　　　**a.** useless or worn out

2. proxy　　　　　　(　　)　　　　**b.** unreasonable or impossible

3. tussle　　　　　　(　　)　　　　**c.** struggle

4. unfeasible　　　　(　　)　　　　**d.** substitute or unofficial

5. defunct　　　　　(　　)　　　　**e.** cry harshly

Summary

次の英文は記事の要約です。下の語群から最も適切な語を 1 つ選び、(　　) 内に記入しなさい。

2-55

20 years after gaining (　　　　　　) from Indonesia, East Timor remains poor. Its offshore gas reserves are (　　　　　) being exploited because of a dispute over the construction of onshore (　　　　　). An agreement with Australia may help to (　　　　　) revenue, but the country desperately needs international funds. This means (　　　　　) for both China and the U.S.

> boost　　hardly　　independence　　infrastructure　　opportunities

東ティモール民主共和国は、正式には2002年5月にインドネシアの占領から独立した。ティモール島は、16世紀にポルトガルによって植民地化され、その後オランダの進出により、1859年に東西に分割され、1913年にオランダとポルトガル間で国境を直線分断することが確定された。その後反乱や蜂起事件が起き、多数の死者や負傷者が出た。第二次世界大戦時にはオランダ軍とオーストラリア軍が保護占領したが、日本軍も占有した。1949年に西ティモールはインドネシアの一部として独立したが、東ティモールにはポルトガルの支配が継続した。1974年から1999年まで東ティモールの領地をめぐりポルトガル、東ティモール、インドネシアの三つ巴戦が続いた。1999年8月国連主導で住民投票が実施され、独立が事実上決定したが、インドネシアが東ティモールに非常事態宣言を発令した。10月には国連暫定行政機構が設立された。

独立後東部住民と西部住民の軋轢、若者の失業率の高さ、政府の独善が原因とされ、5年近く混乱状態にあった。2018年の1人当たりのGDPは2,435ドルで、国民の過半数が1日2ドルで暮らす貧困層である。2007年から11年にかけて平均12.1%にも達する高いGDP成長率を記録したが、ティモール海の海底油田より産出される石油収入による。近年中国が経済支援やインフラ整備で急速に存在感を増している。

Reading

2-56

Twenty years after independence, China eager to help cash-strapped East Timor

cash-strapped：資金の乏しい

CANBERRA/DILI — The runway at the Xanana Gusmao International Airport on East Timor's southern coast is deathly quiet apart from roosters crowing on nearby farms. Built in 2017 to accommodate a $12 billion energy project, it is now
5 barely being used — the only scheduled flight last Saturday was canceled.

Canberra/DILI：（オーストラリアの首都）キャンベラと（東ティモールの首都）ディリ《両方で記事が発信されたことを示す》

Xanana Gusmao International Airport：シャナナ・グスマン国際空港《初代大統領の名に由来》

2-57

Twenty years on from a referendum that brought independence from Indonesia after a brutal quarter-century conflict killed an estimated 100,000 people, East Timor's
10 birthing pains are evident everywhere.

apart from ～：～を除けば

roosters：雄鶏

accommodate ～：～のために便宜を図る

referendum：国民投票、住民投票

The nation on Friday marked 20 years since a U.N.-backed vote ended a decades-long occupation by Indonesian forces and paved the way for it to become an independent nation.

occupation：占領

On Aug. 30, 1999, nearly 80 percent of East Timorese
15 voted to split from Indonesia, which had invaded the former Portuguese colony in 1975. Joy over independence quickly turned to terror as Indonesian security forces and proxy militias went on a scorched-earth rampage. They destroyed infrastructure and forced hundreds of thousands to flee to
20 other parts of Indonesia.

security forces：治安部隊

proxy militias：代理の民兵

scorched-earth rampage：焦土的な乱暴狼藉

2-58

The families of those who died say there has been little justice. "The Indonesian military and militias murdered people who chose to make this an independent nation," said Vital Bere Saldanha, 48, who lost four brothers in the post-
25 vote chaos. "The fight for freedom wasn't easy."

With almost half its 1.2 million people living in poverty, the aging war heroes still in charge are now betting big on a risky energy project that could draw one of the world's youngest nations into a wider geopolitical tussle between the
30 West and China.

in charge：責任ある地位にいる

betting on ～：～に賭ける

geopolitical tussle：地政学的闘争

2-59

Gusmao, the first president, is currently the chief negotiator

of the Greater Sunrise liquefied natural gas development. Fitch Solutions estimates that the project, which has been under negotiation for more than a decade, has enough reserves
35 to yield $50 billion in revenue at today's prices — more than 15 times the country's gross domestic product.

But there is one big problem: Gusmao, 73, has insisted the project be built onshore to create much-needed jobs. For energy giants, that is unfeasible because it requires laying
40 pipeline across a trough to depths of 3,300 meters (11,000 feet). Royal Dutch Shell PLC and ConocoPhillips have given up on the project after more than two decades, selling their stakes back to the government last year. The clock is now ticking for East Timor to find international funding so work
45 can start before its existing oil cash cow — a separate nearby gas field — becomes defunct as soon as 2021.

2-60

The U.S. and China have stepped up competition for influence in emerging economies throughout Asia, with the Trump administration warning countries to avoid becoming
50 indebted to Beijing.

The nation will get some relief with completion of a long-stalled oil and gas maritime boundary treaty with Australia; La'o Hamutuk estimates the previous arrangement cost East Timor $5 billion in lost revenue.

55 The new deal was formalized in Dili on Friday by Australian Prime Minister Scott Morrison. But the need to find more cash is acute.

The Japan Times based on Bloomberg and AFP-JIJI, August 30, 2019

Greater Sunrise liquefied natural gas development：グレーターサンライズ液化天然ガス田開発

Fitch Solutions：フィッチ・ソリューションズ《市場調査会社》

reserves：埋蔵量

yield ～：～を産出する

in revenue：収益

much-needed：切望していた

giants：大手企業

laying ～ to …：～を…に敷設する

trough：〈海底の〉溝

Royal Dutch Shell PLC：ロイアル・ダッチ・シェル《オランダのハーグに本拠地を置くオランダと英国の石油会社》

ConocoPhillips：コノコ・フィリップス《米国ヒューストンに本社を置く総合エネルギー企業；国際石油資本で、スーパーメジャーと呼ばれる6社の一つ》

stakes：〈出資した〉株

The clock is now ticking：残り時間はあとわずか、刻一刻と時間が経過していく

cash cow：ドル箱、金のなる木

defunct：機能していない

as soon as ～：早くも～には

competition for ～：～を巡る競争

get relief：解放される

with completion of ～：～を締結すれば

maritime boundary treaty：海上境界線条約

La'o Hamutuk：ラオ・ハムトゥク《東ティモールの非政府系シンクタンク》

arrangement：合意

cost ～ …：～に…の犠牲を払わせた

$5 billion in lost revenue：50億ドルの損失、収入減

deal：取り決め

Exercises

次の１～５の英文を完成させるために、ａ～ｄの中から最も適切なものを１つ選びなさい。

1. The new airport in East Timor is barely being used because

    a. it is already out of date.

    b. its runway is too short for the latest jets.

    c. the main business centers are on the north coast, not the south.

    d. the nation's economy is stagnant.

2. East Timor voted to get its independence from Indonesia in

    a. 1975.

    b. 1997.

    c. 1999.

    d. 2017.

3. East Timor suffered economic problems upon independence because

    a. the militia and security forces went on a scorched-earth rampage.

    b. most citizens had hoped to remain part of Indonesia.

    c. it was invaded by Portugal.

    d. around 100,000 refugees poured into the country.

4. The problem delaying the gas project favored by former president Gusmao is

    a. his opposition to pipes being laid across the country.

    b. Shell and ConocoPhillips are against laying pipes at great depths.

    c. there is no possibility for international funding now that Shell and ConocoPhillips have withdrawn their support.

    d. Gusmao is too old to deal with modern business practices.

5. East Timor was first colonized by

    a. Portugal.

    b. China.

    c. Indonesia.

    d. Spain.

本文の内容に合致するものに T（True）、合致しないものに F（False）をつけなさい。

(   ) **1.** President Trump has warned countries not to get into debt to Beijing.

(   ) **2.** A separate gas field is expected to remain productive until 2025.

(   ) **3.** East Timor will get some relief from its treaty with Australia.

(   ) **4.** It looks like everything will get better for the country in 2021.

(   ) **5.** The redrawing of sea borders may save the country 5 billion dollars.

Vocabulary

次 の 英 文 は、the Japan Times に 掲 載 さ れ た *Killer crocodiles: Why are more East Timorese being attacked?*『人食いワニ：なぜより多くの東ティモール人が襲われているのか？』の記事の一部です。下の語群から最も適切なものを 1 つ選び、（   ）内に記入しなさい。

Banks, a conservation biologist and Fukuda, a wildlife scientist, took DNA samples from wild crocodiles that had been caught and kept in cages. The Timor samples were then compared against a database of Australian ones to see if there was a (   ) match. Results from the first round of tests give no indication that (   ) reptiles are present in local waters. "They're very much East Timorese. They don't show any evidence of Australian (   )," Banks said.

The animals are (   ) to Timor's creation myth, in which a young boy befriends a crocodile that later dies and is resurrected from the sea in the shape of the mountainous country. "People here see crocodiles as ancestors," said Nina Baris. "According to our beliefs, if a crocodile bites someone then it means we have committed a grave (   )."

This reverence could mean that Timor's sky-high crocodile attacks are actually underreported, and may complicate conservation efforts and strategies to prevent animal-(   ) conflict. "It's not permitted to (   ) crocodiles. If you do, there are serious consequences," Banks said. "So you have to (   ) cultural values against human safety."

ancestry	balance	central	foreign
harm	human	genetic	sin

Unit 24

- ●特殊メイクのカズ・ヒロさん、二度目のアカデミー賞
- ●韓国映画『パラサイト』がアカデミー賞受賞

映画『スキャンダル』での特殊メイクで
二度目のアカデミー賞を受賞した
カズ・ヒロ氏　Photo: ／ロイター／アフロ

映画『パラサイト／半地下の生活』が韓国初のアカデミー賞作品賞
など４部門を受賞し、オスカー像を手にするポン・ジュノ監督

Photo: ED ／ JL ／ A.M.P.A.S. ／ Camera Press ／アフロ

Before you read

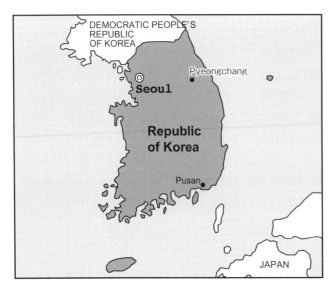

Republic of Korea / South Korea
大韓民国

38度線を挟み朝鮮民主主義人民共和国の統治区域と
対峙する分断国家である

面積	100,210km²（日本の約４分の１）（世界107位）
人口	51,225,000人（世界28位）
民族	大半が朝鮮民族
首都	ソウル
公用語	朝鮮語
宗教	キリスト教・カトリック　20.6%
	キリスト教・プロテスタント　34.5%
	仏教　42.9%
GDP	１兆7,205億ドル（世界10位）
	１人当たりの GDP　33,320ドル（世界28位）
通貨	ウォン
政体	共和制
識字率	99%

次の1〜5の語句の説明として最も近いものをa〜eから1つ選び、（　）内に記入しなさい。

1. mete out　　　　（　　）　　a. artificial body parts

2. prosthetics　　　（　　）　　b. sound clear and loud

3. quench　　　　　（　　）　　c. widening gap between two extremes

4. ring out　　　　 （　　）　　d. give or dispense forcefully

5. polarization　　 （　　）　　e. satisfy

Summary

次の英文は記事の要約です。下の語群から最も適切な語を1つ選び、（　　）内に記入しなさい。

2-61

After several (　　　　　　　), Japanese-born makeup artist Kazu Hiro has won (　　　　　　　) Oscar — for his work on "Bombshell". Hiro is (　　　　　　　) for his use of prosthetics. Japan's (　　　　　　　) has also gained Hollywood success. The social (　　　　　　　) "Parasite" was not only the first Korean film, but also the first foreign language film, to take the Oscar for best picture.

another　　famous　　neighbor　　nominations　　satire

2020年2月9日に第92回のアカデミー賞授賞式が行われ、作品賞と監督賞、脚本賞、国際長編映画賞の4冠に輝いた「Parasite パラサイト 半地下の家族」が受賞した。英語以外の外国語映画がアカデミー賞の作品賞を受賞するのは、史上初である。韓国映画が受賞するのも初めてのことである。

ブラック・コメディ・スリラー映画「パラサイト」は、半地下に暮らす貧しい一家が、高台の豪邸に住む裕福な一家と出会うことから始まる。韓国における格差社会を批判しつつも娯楽性の高い作品で、脚本の良さ、登場人物の悪さ・ユニークさは、字幕という言葉の壁を乗り越えることができる。アメリカ映画界は、本格的に多様性を受け入れたことを示している。

米国・カナダ合作の映画「Bombshell スキャンダル」の特殊メイクを担当した日本生まれのカズ・ヒロ（辻一弘から改名）が、メーキャップ・ヘアスタイリング賞を他の2人と共に受賞した。「スキャンダル」はニュース放送局で起こったセクハラ疑惑を描いたもので、実在の女性キャスターと瓜二つに変身させた。撮影は40日程度続き、特殊メイクには毎日約3時間も要したという。

Reading

2-62

Makeup artist Kazu Hiro wins second Oscar for work on 'Bombshell'

Makeup artist Kazu Hiro on Monday picked up an Oscar for best makeup and hairstyling at the 92nd Academy Awards in Los Angeles.

Hiro — formerly known in Japan as Kazuhiro Tsuji — 5 was nominated alongside Anne Morgan and Vivian Baker for his work on "Bombshell," a biographical drama about a group of female Fox News employees who set out to expose the sexual harassment meted out by the company's CEO.

2-63

Hiro, 50, has made a name for himself in the art of 10 prosthetics, having created visual effects for such films as "Men in Black" (1997), "Planet of the Apes" (2001) and "Hellboy" (2004). He also received Oscar nominations for "Click" (2006) and "Norbit" (2007), but had to wait until 2018 for his first win.

15 His work transforming Gary Oldman into British wartime Prime Minister Winston Churchill for 2017's "Darkest Hour" saw him pick up an award alongside David Malinowski and Lucy Sibbick the next year for best makeup and hairstyling.

2-64

Hiro and his colleagues were nominated alongside the 20 makeup and hairstyling staffs for the films "Joker," "Judy," "Maleficent: Mistress of Evil" and "1917."

A leading artist in ultrarealistic sculptures and prosthetics, Hiro was born in Kyoto in 1969 and later moved to Los Angeles to pursue film work. His first production was the 25 1989 Japanese film "Sweet Home" by Kiyoshi Kurosawa.

He obtained U.S. citizenship in 2019, upon which he changed his name.

The Japan Times, February 10, 2020

Oscar：オスカー像《アカデミー賞受賞者に授与される賞品》

"Bombshell"：邦題『スキャンダル』

Kazuhiro Tsuji：辻一弘

Fox News：FOX ニュース《米国のニュース専門放送局》

CEO：最高経営責任者（chief executive officer）

made a name for himself in 〜：〜で名を挙げた

prosthetics：プロテーゼ、補綴学

"Planet of the Apes"：邦題『猿の惑星』

"Click"：邦題『もしも明日が選べたら』

"Norbit"：邦題『マッド・ファット・ワイフ』

"Darkest Hour"：邦題『ウィンストン・チャーチル／ヒトラーから世界を救った男』

"Judy"：邦題『ジュディ 虹の彼方に』

"Maleficent: Mistress of Evil"：邦題『マレフィセント 2 悪の女王』

"1917"：邦題『1917 命をかけた伝令』

Kiyoshi Kurosawa：黒沢清《1955年生まれの映画監督、脚本家、小説家》

Oscar for 'Parasite' Quenches Koreans' Long Thirst for Recognition

SEOUL, South Korea — Much of the world knows South Korea by its cultural products, including its increasingly popular movies, TV dramas and K-pop performers like BTS and Psy. Now the country has received once-unthinkable
35 validation of its artistic achievement: a best-picture Oscar.

On Monday, the director Bong Joon Ho's "Parasite" a genre-defying film about class warfare, won that award and three other Oscars, including best director. It was a historic moment for both the Oscars and South Koreans: "Parasite" was
40 the first ever foreign language film to win the top Academy Award, and for South Korea, it was a moment of collective national pride.

In office buildings in downtown Seoul, where people were watching live streams of the awards ceremony, cheers rang
45 out on Monday morning. The South Korean president kicked off his staff meeting with a round of applause for the director. Local media sent out news flashes.

As soon as "Parasite" hit the screens last May, it resonated with South Koreans because it used a masterful mix of comedy,
50 satire and violence to describe one of the country's biggest social and political issues: widening income inequality and the despair it has generated, especially among young South Koreans.

"People around the world could relate to the polarization it
55 describes," said Huh Eun, a retired college professor in Seoul and a fan of Mr. Bong's films. "The film was an extended metaphor for how the deepening rich-poor gap in advanced capitalist societies breeds blind hatred and crimes."

The New York Times, February 10, 2020

'Parasite'：邦題『パラサイト 半地下の家族』

Quenches 〜：〜を癒す、和らげる

Thirst for Recognition：（自分が）認められたいとの渇望

BTS：《旧名称は「防弾少年団」という男性ヒップホップ・グループ》

Psy：《発音は「サイ」；歌手としては「江南スタイル」が世界的ヒット》

validation：証明（書）

Bong Joon Ho：ポン・ジュノ

class warfare：階級闘争

top Academy Award：アカデミー賞作品賞を指す

live streams：ライブ配信

applause：拍手喝采

sent out news flashes：ニュース速報を送信した

hit the screens：公開された

resonated with 〜：〜の間で共感を呼んだ

satire：風刺

income inequality：所得不平等

despair：絶望

relate to 〜：〜を自分に事のように感じる

polarization：二極化

Huh Eun：ホ・ウン

metaphor for 〜：〜を示す暗喩

breeds 〜：〜の原因となる

blind hatred：無思慮な憎悪

Exercises

Multiple Choice

次の１～３の英文を完成させ、４～５の英文の質問に答えるために、a～dの中から最も適切なものを１つ選びなさい。

1. Kazu Hiro received an Oscar at the 92nd Academy Award for

    a. best director for the movie "Parasite."

    b. screenplay for "Bombshell."

    c. makeup and hairstyling for "Bombshell."

    d. makeup and hairstyling for "Parasite."

2. Kazu Hiro won an Oscar in 2018 for makeup and hairstyling for the movie

    a. "Planet of the Apes."

    b. "Darkest Hour."

    c. "Men in Black."

    d. "Click."

3. The polarization depicted through satire and violence in "Parasite" was appreciated by

    a. South Koreans of the older generation only.

    b. most of the world including South Korea.

    c. most people except for the Koreans.

    d. almost all Asians but few Europeans or Americans.

4. How many Oscars for 'Parasite' did Bong Joon Ho win?

    a. Four.

    b. Three.

    c. Two.

    d. One.

5. What distinguished "Parasite" from other Oscar-winning movies?

    a. It was the shortest running movie to win the Best Picture Award.

    b. It was the first foreign-language movie to win the Best Picture Oscar.

    c. It was the longest running picture to win the Best Picture Award.

    d. It was the first comedy to win Best Picture.

本文の内容に合致するものに T (True)、合致しないものに F (False) をつけなさい。

(   ) **1.** Mr. Kazu Hiro became a U.S. citizen and changed his name in 2018.

(   ) **2.** Mr. Hiro is known for his ultrarealistic sculptures and prosthetics.

(   ) **3.** The picture "Parasite" and Bong Joon Ho won the Oscars for Best Picture and Best Director.

(   ) **4.** Few people in South Korea felt national pride about this award.

(   ) **5.** The Oscar for "Parasite" was surprising because South Korea is not well-known for its cultural exports.

Vocabulary

次の１〜８は、「insects 昆虫」に関する英文です。日本文に合わせて（　　　）内に最も適切な昆虫名を下の語群から１つ選び、記入しなさい。

1. 彼に嫌味を言って追い払った。
   I sent him off with a (　　　　　) in his ear.

2. ドキドキしている。
   I have (　　　　　) in my stomach.

3. かぶと虫に似ていると言われる。
   They say I look like a (　　　　　).

4. 社会のやっかい者のようだ。
   He seems to be a (　　　　　) of society.

5. 旅行に取りつかれている。
   I am bitten by the travel (　　　　　).

6. すごく陽気だった。
   I was as merry as a (　　　　　).

7. 不安でイライラしている。
   I have (　　　　　) in my pants.

8. 妙な考えにとりつかれている。
   I have a (　　　　　) in my bonnet.

ants	bee	beetle	butterflies
bug	cricket	flea	parasite

●カルロス・ゴーンの大脱走劇

2019年3月、保釈されて東京拘置所を出る日産
自動車の前会長カルロス・ゴーン被告

Photo: Kyodo News

Before you read

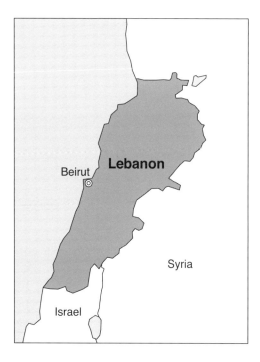

Lebanese Republic
レバノン共和国
面積　10,452km²（岐阜県とほぼ同じ）（世界161位）
首都・最大都市　ベイルート
公用語　アラビア語（フランス語と英語も通用）
人口　6,856,000人（世界108位）
民族　アラブ人　95%
　　　アルメニア人　4%
宗教　キリスト教（マロン派 ／ ギリシャ正教 ／ ギ
　　　リシャ・カトリック ／ カトリック ／
　　　アルメニア正教）40.4%
　　　イスラム教　54%
　　　ドゥルーズ派　5.6%
識字率　87.4%
GDP　563.72億ドル（世界82位）
　　　1人当たりのGDP　9,251ドル（世界76位）
通貨　レバノン・ポンド
政体　共和制

次の１～５の語句の説明として最も近いものをａ～ｅから１つ選び、（　）内に記入しなさい。

1. fugitive	（　）	**a.**	active
2. procedural	（　）	**b.**	a person escaping from the law
3. hands-on	（　）	**c.**	disobey or violate
4. infringe	（　）	**d.**	hide
5. conceal	（　）	**e.**	administrative or bureaucratic

Summary

　次の英文は記事の要約です。下の語群から最も適切な語を１つ選び、（　）内に記入しなさい。

2-67

　　Facing (　　　　　) from Nissan, and (　　　　　) who win almost every case, Carlos Ghosn made escape plans that seemed (　　　　) to succeed. In the relaxed days before New Year, with private security forces temporarily (　　　　), he took a train to Kansai Airport and flew off in a private jet, (　　　　) in a case too large for the x-ray machines.

hidden　　hostility　　prosecutors　　unlikely　　withdrawn

　　1954年ブラジル生まれの Carlos Ghosn カルロス・ゴーンは45歳の時、日産自動車の最高執行責任者に就任した。その後、日産自動車の社長兼最高経営責任者、ルノーの取締役会長兼最高経営責任者、ルノー・日産アライアンスの会長兼最高経営責任者に就任した。
　　カルロスの祖父は、13歳のときレバノンからブラジルに移住した。父親はブラジル生まれでナイジェリア出身のレバノン人女性と結婚した。カルロスが６歳のとき、母親と３人の姉妹と共にレバノンのベイルートに転居し、小・中学校教育はベイルートで受け、高校はパリで学び、1974年、20歳でエリート養成校 Ecole Polytechnique を卒業し、24歳で Ecole des Mines de Paris で工学博士を取得した。24歳でタイヤメーカーのミシュランに入社し、30歳で南米ミシュラン最高執行責任者、36歳で北米の最高経営責任者に昇格した。1996年にルノーの上席副社長にヘッドハンティングされ、1999年にルノーと日産の資本提携後、ルノーの役職も兼任しながら日産の最高執行責任者に就任した。
　　2018年11月、東京地検特捜部により金融商品取引法違反容疑で逮捕された。19年４月に特別背任の容疑で４度目の逮捕となったが、再度保釈された。同年12月29日に海外渡航を禁じた裁判所の保釈条件を破り、日本を秘密裏に出国、プライベートジェットでトルコを経由し、31日の朝ベイルート国際空港に到着した。

Reading

The Great Escape: How Carlos Ghosn became the world's most famous fugitive

fugitive：逃亡犯人

SINGAPORE / LONDON / TOKYO / PARIS — Ghosn's prospects of proving his innocence in Japan were dismal. Prosecutors there win more than 99 percent of the cases they try and enjoy a wide range of procedural advantages. Against
5 Ghosn, who was facing potential sentences of more than a decade in prison, they had an even greater-than-usual asset: the full co-operation of Nissan, which had repeatedly made clear its determination to see him convicted and had provided a huge trove of documents as well as hands-on investigative
10 assistance.

prospects：見通し
innocence：無実
dismal：暗い
Prosecutors：検察官
cases they try：彼らが裁判
にかける訴訟（事例）
enjoy 〜：〜に恵まれている
sentences：判決
asset：有用なもの
convicted：有罪宣告を受ける
hands-on：現場での

Ghosn, however, had another option — a desperate play, months in the planning, that might restore some portion of his freedom if everything went right, or send him straight back to a 7-meter-square (75-foot-square) cell in Tokyo if any aspect
15 went awry.

desperate play：一か八か
の捨て身の行動

cell：独房
any aspect went awry：あ
る局面で失敗したら

On its face, it must have seemed like a ridiculous idea.

On its face：一見

Yet there was a clear window of opportunity: New Year's, when government offices can close for more than a week and even the most hard-boiled prosecutors and police
20 detectives take time off to be with their families. His lawyers had recently threatened to file a complaint against a private security company hired by Nissan to follow him, claiming it was infringing illegally on his rights. According to a person familiar with the situation, the company's agents had backed
25 off as a result — at least temporarily.

police detectives：刑事

file a complaint against
〜：〜を告訴する
follow 〜：〜を監視する
infringing on 〜：〜を侵害
している
agents：スパイ

If Ghosn was going to escape, this was the moment to do it. But he needed the right help.

In the shadowy world of private-security contractors, Michael Taylor was a swashbuckler who stood out. He
30 protected powerful people and companies, secretly helped the U.S. government investigate crimes, and admitted breaking

swashbuckler：無法者、悪漢

the law himself.

For the Ghosn operation, Taylor had a partner, a Lebanese-born man named George-Antoine Zayek.

35 On the morning of Sunday, Dec. 29, Taylor and Zayek arrived in a Bombardier Global Express Jet — a plane with a range of more than 11,000 kilometers (6,800 miles) — at the private-jet terminal of Kansai International Airport, a busy hub built on an artificial island near Osaka. There were also
40 two large black cases on board, according to people familiar with the flight who asked not to be identified.

Later the same day, according to security camera footage reported on by Japanese media, Ghosn walked out the front door of his house, wearing a hat and a surgical-style face
45 mask. He then took a bullet train from Tokyo's Shinagawa Station to Osaka at about 4:30 p.m. local time and, after the journey, took a cab to a hotel near the airport, the network NTV reported.

Outbound passengers at the private terminal aren't exempt
50 from passport control, and according to people familiar with airport operations, there were customs and immigration officials present before the Bombardier's departure. But Ghosn wasn't boarding as an official passenger. He was, apparently, cargo, concealed in a large black case that, according to the
55 people, was too big to fit into the airport's X-ray machines. With nothing obviously amiss, the jet was in the air by 11:10 p.m.

The Japan Times based on Bloomberg, January 8, 2020

operation：作戦

Bombardier Global Express Jet：《カナダのボンバルディア・エアロスペース社開発の大型ビジネスジェット機》
range：航続距離
busy hub：離発着便の多いハブ空港

asked not to be identified：匿名希望の

bullet train：新幹線

NTV：日本テレビ《Nippon Television》
Outbound：出国する
exempt from 〜：〜を免除される
passport control：出入国審査
customs and immigration officials：税関・出入国管理局職員
present：立ち会う
cargo：貨物
the people：関係者

amiss：間違った

Exercises

Multiple Choice

次の１〜３の英文の質問に答え、４〜５の英文を完成させるために、ａ〜ｄの中から最も適切なものを１つ選びなさい。

1. If convicted, how much prison time might Ghosn have to serve?

    a. Ten years.
    b. Fifteen years.
    c. Twenty years.
    d. Twenty-five years.

2. How did Ghosn get on the plane?

    a. He was placed in a large cargo box that was too large to fit through the x-ray machine.
    b. He walked onto the plane disguised as a woman.
    c. He took a taxi to the airport and met his 'handlers.'
    d. The article does not go into any detail about this mystery.

3. Who assisted Ghosn in arranging plans for his escape from the country?

    a. His family members.
    b. Michael Taylor and George-Antoine Zayek.
    c. Several associates from Nissan who were "in his corner."
    d. A private security company that was hired to follow him.

4. Nissan seems to have been

    a. very keen to cooperate fully with the prosecution.
    b. willing to provide documents in their possession to get Ghosn convicted.
    c. hoping Ghosn would stand trial in Japan.
    d. taking all of the above stances in the period before Ghosn escaped.

5. Ghosn's chances of being acquitted are said to be

    a. excellent.
    b. fifty-fifty.
    c. gloomy.
    d. somewhat slim.

True or False

本文の内容に合致するものに T（True）、合致しないものに F（False）をつけなさい。

(   )   **1.** The conviction rate of legal cases in Japan is at least 99%.

(   )   **2.** The plane took off from the private jet terminal at Kansai Airport.

(   )   **3.** Michael Taylor is described in the article as a swashbuckler, a word usually used for pirates.

(   )   **4.** The plan to escape Japan was made very quickly.

(   )   **5.** Ghosn managed to avoid passport control by walking onto the plane in disguise.

Vocabulary

次の英文は、the Japan Times に掲載された *Once a hero in Japan, Carlos Ghosn's news conference unlikely to restore his image*『日本で英雄だったカルロス・ゴーンの記者会見も彼のイメージ回復にはならないようだ』の記事の一部です。下の語群から最も適切なものを1つ選び、（　　）内に記入しなさい。

In an extraordinary news conference 14 months in the making, Carlos Ghosn (　　　　　) Nissan Motor Co. executives, Japanese prosecutors and the nation's (　　　　　) system in what was a watershed moment for a corporate crime drama that has made global headlines and stirred talks of a Hollywood production.

By (　　　　　) to Lebanon and thus (　　　　　) himself from the legal risks that would have come from speaking to the media in Japan, the former Nissan chairman was granted his long-held wish to provide his own account in his own words. He made full use of the opportunity – speaking for an hour before (　　　　　) questions from reporters – and covered topics including harrowing accounts of his detention, while also (　　　　　) Nissan executives that he says had a role in bringing him down.

While international media has focused much of its coverage on criticisms of the Japanese criminal justice system, domestic media outlets have been more critical of Ghosn (　　　　　) bail conditions and leaving the country without facing trial.

answering	fleeing	freeing	justice
lambasted	outing	violating	

Unit 26

● 渋野日奈子、全英女子オープンゴルフ優勝でメジャーデビュー

全英女子オープンゴルフで優勝トロフィーを掲げ、ほほ笑む渋野日向子選手

Photo: REX ／アフロ

Before you read

　1 〜 10 の「A Golf Course」の呼称に該当するものをイラスト a 〜 j の中から 1 つ選び、（　　　）内に記入しなさい。

1. club house　（　　）
2. golfer　（　　）
3. caddie　（　　）
4. fairway　（　　）
5. club　（　　）
6. tee　（　　）
7. bunker　（　　）
8. flag　（　　）
9. green　（　　）
10. rough　（　　）

次の１〜５の語の説明として最も近いものをa〜eから１つ選び、（　）内に記入しなさい。

1. jaunt	（　）	**a.** trip or adventure
2. endearing	（　）	**b.** echo
3. rigidity	（　）	**c.** stiff attitudes or rules
4. reverberate	（　）	**d.** heartwarming
5. linger	（　）	**e.** remain in the mind or in a place

次の英文は記事の要約です。下の語群から最も適切な語を１つ選び、（　）内に記入しなさい。

2-73

　Hinako Shibuno played brilliant golf to (　　　　　) American Lizette Salas by just one stroke at the British Open. She showed (　　　　) of the nervousness she later claimed to have felt. Rather, she (　　　　) fans with her relaxed and friendly attitude. Salas had hoped at least for a (　　　　　). But when Shibuno holed her final putt her hopes were (　　　　).

> beat　　charmed　　dashed　　none　　play-off

　2019年８月の全英女子オープンを制して「シンデレラストーリー」を体現した渋野日奈子21歳の登場が、ゴルフ市場そして女子選手の環境に大きな変化をもたらしている。2020年春、新型コロナウイルス感染拡大よる国内外のゴルフツアー休止が続いているが、女子新人選手らのスポンサー契約が相次ぎ、次の「しぶこ」争奪戦が繰り広げられている。スター選手の存在は、大会中継の視聴率、ゴルフ関連市場の売り上げに大きな効果をもたらしている。

　1998年岡山市生まれの渋野日奈子選手は、小学校２年生の夏休みにゴルフと出会った。彼女の父親は砲丸投げと円盤投げ、母親はやり投げの選手だった。11歳のとき「岡山県ジュニアゴルフ選手権競技」で３位、中学１年、２年、３年「中学生・女子の部」で３連覇を果たした。高校１年の「中国女子アマチュア選手権」で優勝。翌年「全国高等学校ゴルフ選手権大会」の女子団体戦で優勝した。高校卒業後の2017年日本女子プロゴルフ協会のプロテストに落ちたが、18年７月末に14位で合格した。

　2019年５月「ワールドレディスチャンピオンシップサロンパスカップ」で20歳178日の大会史上最年少優勝となった。19年８月の海外初試合「AIG 全英女子オープン」通算18アンダー、初出場初優勝でメジャー大会を飾った。「スマイリング・シンデレラ」として注目を浴びた。

Reading

Hinako Shibuno wins Women's British Open on major debut

Hinako Shibuno captured hearts and minds long before she decided to take delivery of the Women's British Open trophy for good measure. The 20-year-old, who until this event had been outside Japan only once — that jaunt to Thailand did not
5 even involve any golf — produced one of the most endearing stories of this year by holing out from 18ft to claim this title.

Shibuno, nicknamed "the Smiling Cinderella", shall indeed go to the ball. She was having one for four days. Her golf, which propelled her to 18 under par, was exemplary. Her
10 infectious attitude proved a revelation; in the heat of battle, she was highfiving spectators and waving to adoring galleries in a manner far from customary in a sport beset by rigidity.

It felt altogether fitting that there was one perfect moment delivered with the final putt of the tournament. Had the ball
15 not banged into the back of the cup, it seemed destined to roll several feet past.

Fear not, Cinderella. Shibuno's back nine of 31 on her major championship debut afforded her a one-shot victory over Lizette Salas.

20 "I feel like I'm going to vomit," said Shibuno, suggesting anxiety that was not at all apparent. "Contending at a tournament like this is nerve-racking but I was determined to enjoy it."

Shibuno looked destined to fall short. She made a double
25 bogey at the 3rd and played the front nine in 37. The inward half at Woburn was kind to Shibuno all week — she played it in a four-round total of minus 18.

As Shibuno celebrated, it was impossible not to feel sympathy for Salas. The American found herself an unwanted
30 centre of attention at this tournament in 2015, owing to its hosting by Donald Trump's Turnberry resort. Salas was

Women's British Open：全英女子オープンゴルフ（大会）

take delivery of ～：～を受け取る

for good measure：おまけとして

endearing：心和む

holing out from 18ft：18フィート（約5メートル）からのパットを沈めて競技を終了

claim this title：優勝する

ball：舞踏会《シンデレラからの連想で社交界（メジャートーナメント）デビュー》

having one：それを大いに楽しむ《one は the ball》

exemplary：賞賛すべきもの

infectious attitude：見ている人もつられて笑顔になるような微笑みなどの振る舞い

revelation：驚くべきこと

beset by rigidity：堅苦しさに取り囲まれた

Had the ball …：《if を用いない仮定法過去完了》

back nine：後半9ホール、インコース

one-shot victory over ～：～に対する一打差の勝利

Contending：戦う、競う

nerve-racking：緊張する、イライラする

fall short：優勝に手が届かない

the 3rd：3番ホール

Woburn：ウォバーンゴルフ場

it：後半の9ホール《inward half を指す》

Donald Trump's Turnberry resort：トランプ・ターンベリー・ゴルフコース《スコットランドのサウス・エアシャーにある》

bombarded by news outlets then and by her own admission felt desperately uncomfortable after the then-US president elect had made disparaging remarks about Mexicans. Salas, a
35 US Solheim Cup player, is of Mexican descent.

Salas was on the verge of regarding the British Open in altogether different light. Playing two groups in front of Shibuno, she stood over a 5ft putt on the 18th green with the chance to move to 18 under. The birdie attempt remained
40 above ground.

Her hopes of possible salvation via a play-off were ended by Shibuno's brilliance. The roar as the Japanese converted reverberated to the practice putting green, where Salas was preparing for potential extra holes. These kind of defeats tend
45 to linger, especially for a 30-year-old without a major title.

In tears, Salas admitted there was a "sting" attached to what transpired. "I told myself: 'You got this. You're made for this,'" said Salas of her fateful moment. "I put a good stroke on it. I'm not going to lie. I was nervous. I haven't
50 been in that position in a long time. I gave it a good stroke, I controlled all my thoughts, it just didn't drop. So congrats to our winner."

The Guardian, August 4, 2019

then-president elect：当時の次期大統領
made disparaging remarks about ～：～を中傷する発言をした
US Solheim Cup player：ソルハイムカップ米国代表選手《女子ゴルフのヨーロッパツアーとアメリカツアーの代表選手による団体対抗戦》
on the verge of ～：今にも～しようとして
remained above ground：地面に残っていた→カップに入らなかった
brilliance：優れた才能
the Japanese converted：ラグビーで日本チームが（追加）得点した
reverberated to ～：～に反響して鳴り響いた
extra holes：プレーオフ
sting：心の痛み
You got this：よく聞いて
You're made for this：あなたにはこれがお似合いよ
put a good stroke：パットは良かったわ
that position：メジャー大会で優勝を争うような状況
controlled all my thoughts：全神経を集中させたわ
drop：カップの中に入る
congrats to ～：～におめでとうと言うわ

Exercises

Multiple Choice

次の1～5の英文を完成させるために、a～dの中から最も適切なものを1つ選びなさい。

1. Hinako Shibuno has

    a. a rigid manner.

    b. a vague attitude.

    c. a friendly appearance.

    d. an ingenious approach.

2. Her nickname is

    a. Princess Leah.

    b. Smiling Cinderella.

    c. Sweetheart Girl.

    d. Golden Golfer.

3. Before Britain, Hinako had been outside of Japan

    a. many times.

    b. just once, for a golf tournament.

    c. for regular holidays to Thailand.

    d. only once.

4. This time she won the

    a. British Women's Open.

    b. U.S. Open.

    c. Nabisco Classic.

    d. Solheim Cup.

5. To win the tournament Shibuno

    a. had a double bogey.

    b. made an 18 feet putt on the 18th.

    c. completely overcame any nervousness.

    d. remained quiet and avoided interacting with the crowd.

本文の内容に合致するものに T（True）、合致しないものに F（False）をつけなさい。

(   ) **1.** Salas was gracious and congratulated Shibuno on a fantastic win.

(   ) **2.** President Trump criticized Salas's character.

(   ) **3.** Shibuno's golf was exemplary.

(   ) **4.** Many spectators felt Salas's disappointment because in 2018 she was upset by Trump's comments.

(   ) **5.** Salas is younger than Shibuno.

Vocabulary

次の１～８はゴルフ用語です。該当する英語説明文を下の a ～ h の中から１つ選び、（   ）内に入れなさい。

1. albatross   (   )
2. birdie   (   )
3. bogey   (   )
4. eagle   (   )
5. grand slam   (   )
6. hole in one   (   )
7. par   (   )
8. triple bogey   (   )

a. a hole played in two strokes under par
b. a hole played in one stroke under par
c. a hole played one stroke over par
d. using only one stroke
e. standard score for a hole or a course
f. a hole played three strokes under par
g. a hole played three strokes over par
h. winning all the golf's major championships in the same calendar year

ニュースメディアの英語

―演習と解説2021年度版―

検印
省略

Ⓒ2021年1月31日　初版発行

編著者　　　　　　　高橋　優身

伊藤　典子

Richard　Powell

発行者　　　　　　　原　　雅　久

発行所　　　　　株式会社朝日出版社

101-0065　東京都千代田区西神田3-3-5
電話（03）3239-0271
FAX（03）3239-0479
e-mail: text-e@asahipress.com
振替口座　00140-2-46008
組版・製版／信毎書籍印刷株式会社

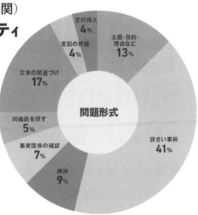